DATE DUE

			PRINTED IN U.S.A.

Linkin **tion

Parlis

Ending Remediation:
Linking ESL and Content in Higher Education

Sarah Benesch
Editor

Teachers of English to Speakers of Other Languages

Typeset in Mergenthaler Caledonia by
Graftec Corporation, Washington, DC
and lithographed by
Pantagraph Printing, Bloomington, IL

Staff Editor: Helen Kornblum
Editorial Assistants: Daniela Cuomo
Juana Hopkins

Library of Congress Catalog No. 88-50723
ISBN 0-939791-33-1

Preface

This thematic volume grew out of a colloquium on Models of English for Academic Purposes presented at the 1986 TESOL Convention in Anaheim, California. Participants were invited by the TESOL Publications Committee to solicit other papers and to submit these and their own for review. Two of the papers, those of Benesch and Brooks, were part of the original colloquium. With the addition of four solicited papers, the theme of the volume changed to the theory and practice of linking content and language instruction in ESL higher education.

Several people have contributed to this project over the last two years. First, I would like to thank Diane Larsen-Freeman, former Chair of the TESOL Publications Committee, for her support and feedback. I would also like to thank Julia Frank-McNeil, former TESOL Director of Publications, who repeatedly made herself available for questions about production, and Helen Kornblum, current Director, whose care and efficiency allowed us to meet the publication deadline. Next, I would like to thank my colleagues at the College of Staten Island, Professors Ortiz, Hartman, and Cornwell, for encouraging my interest in the topic of linking content and language instruction. Finally I would like to thank the authors, Professors Smoke, Brooks, Snow, Brinton, Hirsch, Guyer, and Peterson, who submitted their drafts on time and willingly revised and edited their papers in order to share research and ideas with TESOL's members.

Sarah Benesch
College of Staten Island,
City University of New York

Contents

Introduction

At the 1987 TESOL Convention, the Committee on Professional Standards passed a resolution calling for the granting of credit for ESL courses in institutions of higher education. ESL courses, the resolution states, are as intellectually demanding as the foreign language courses for which native college students receive full academic credit and should therefore be credit-bearing. The resolution recognizes ESL instruction as foreign language instruction, rather than remediation. It also recognizes that nonnative students are made to feel separate, ghettoized, when they are required to take noncredit ESL courses before they can enroll in content courses.

The resolution was passed at a time when state boards of higher education across the country were removing or reducing credit for remedial courses, making ESL college courses especially vulnerable because they have traditionally been labeled remedial. ESL professionals in higher education have responded to this challenge by lobbying for academic credit for their courses and by reconsidering what constitutes academic, college-level second language learning.

One positive outcome of the threat to ESL college credit may be a shift from remedial, skills-oriented ESL instruction, which presents language as a set of discrete bits of knowledge such as "the sentence," "the paragraph," and "-ed endings," toward communicative and whole language approaches (Widdowson, 1978; Morley, 1987). These approaches, which call for students to read and discuss full-length texts (Krashen, 1985) and to write and revise essays (Raimes, 1985; Zamel, 1982, 1983), are more appropriate for college courses than is the remedial approach which views students as patients who are deficient in "basic skills" and must be cured before they are asked to read, discuss, and write about whole texts. Research on teaching grammar has not demonstrated a transfer of learning from decontextualized language exercises to communicative situations (Hartwell, 1985). Perhaps this information will convince more ESL faculty that it is sound policy to invite students to read unabridged texts and to accept their tentative, initial responses while providing opportunities for the development of more critical and articulate responses.

To move away from a skills or remedial approach to teaching is

1

not to deny that our students need language courses. It allows us
to offer a more challenging, integrated curriculum and to see our
students as healthy, intelligent human beings rather than as deficient individuals needing remedies. As Rose (1985) argues:

> Remediation. It is time to abandon this troublesome
> metaphor. To do so will not blind us to the fact that many
> entering students are not adequately prepared to take on
> the demands of university work. In fact, it will help us
> perceive these young people and the work they do in
> ways that foster appropriate notions about language devel-
> opment and use, that establish a framework for more
> rigorous and comprehensive analysis of their difficulties,
> and that do not perpetuate the raree show of allowing
> them entrance to the academy while, in various symbolic
> ways, denying them full participation. (p. 357)

Nonnative students should be welcomed as members of the
academic community. They have learned a first language and have
thus demonstrated that they do not lack linguistic ability or skills;
they do need experience and practice using their second language.
They should be offered ESL instruction because, unlike their
native counterparts, they have not had twelve years of schooling in
English. And, like many of their native counterparts, they need
practice in listening to, speaking, writing, and reading English in
an academic context to ensure their continued membership in the
community.
    The papers collected in this volume represent one form that the
shift from remedial to college-level ESL instruction has taken.
Four of the papers, those of Brinton and Snow, Benesch, Hirsch,
and Guyer and Peterson, describe programs that link ESL and
content instruction, thereby moving ESL out of the ghetto and
into the mainstream. Though the solutions presented are somewhat different, they share the underlying assumption that ESL
instruction in higher education should mediate between students'
previous experiences with English and formal learning and the
new linguistic, cognitive, social, and cultural demands of studying
content in an American college in the target language.
    The first article provides a rationale for rethinking how ESL is
taught at the college level. Smoke describes her survey of 198
nonnative students who had completed their required developmental writing courses and were enrolled in regular academic
programs. Her purpose was to discover whether these students
felt that developmental courses had prepared them for college

work and what, if anything, they would have changed or added to that instruction. Smoke found that while 97% of the students surveyed agreed that their English had improved as a result of taking ESL courses, only 18% felt that these courses had prepared them for American college work.

Smoke also found that many of her subjects, after completing their developmental courses, had strategies for staying in college while avoiding using English: They took courses pass/fail; they enrolled in first-year courses in their native language; they chose only science and math courses; and they stayed away from courses in which writing was assigned, including some in their major and the required freshman composition course. These students lacked the confidence to choose from the full array of course offerings, even though they would eventually have to enroll in a greater range of courses to graduate. Smoke calls on ESL faculty to provide their students with experiences in using language to learn in particular content areas, including reading a variety of texts, writing research papers, listening to lectures and taking notes, and giving oral presentations. Such activities in ESL courses will prepare students for a comprehensive liberal arts education. Smoke also recommends the creation of linked courses to bridge the gap between developmental and college-level courses.

Brooks describes an effort by ESL faculty to discover two things about nonnative college students: What demands do they face in content courses in a core curriculum, and what expectations do they raise in core faculty? The prevailing assumption found among content teachers is that once ESL students have passed through the ESL sequence, they ought to be proficient and confident users of English.] Interestingly, at the college where the study took place, ESL students take language and core courses concurrently so that, in theory, the responsibility for language instruction is shared by content and language teachers alike. Because language education—reading, writing, and discussion—can not be separated from content teaching, it is the domain of all faculty members. Yet, Brooks found a widespread perception of ESL as a service course which should take care of language learning once and for all. One of the implications of Brooks' article is that we need greater communication between content and ESL faculty to reconcile our ideas about what counts as knowledge, teaching, and learning in higher education and to define our respective and mutual roles in educating nonnative students.

Many American colleges have recognized the desirability of collaboration between ESL faculty and our colleagues in the disciplines. It is an outstanding feature of four linkage programs described

in the other papers in this volume. Collaboration ranges from
preservice planning meetings among administrators, language teachers, content teachers, counselors, and tutors at UCLA (Brinton
and Snow), to weekly curriculum meetings among content, reading, and writing teachers at the College of Staten Island (Benesch),
to ESL teachers' attending the content classes linked to their
language courses at Hostos Community College (Hirsch) and
Macalester College (Guyer and Peterson).

Although there are similarities in these four programs, each has
a unique structure based on differing instructional philosophies
and goals. At UCLA, the primary purpose of instruction is to
introduce freshmen, native and nonnative, to the academic, social,
and recreational complexity of university life. Along with pairing
language and content courses, those who developed the UCLA
model included tutoring and counseling components to ease student adjustment.

The philosophy of the Freshman Workshop Program at the
College of Staten Island is that not only incoming students but also
their teachers need to become aware of the differences between
studying in high school and in college. Two components of the
program, the preservice training seminar and the weekly in-service
meetings, were designed to offer language and content teachers
ways to deal collaboratively with the difficulties experienced by
freshmen in college classes.

The model developed and described by Hirsch is based on the
notion that the language of the classroom and of textbooks must be
demystified if nonnative students are to compete with their native
counterparts. In the Hostos program, ESL students are given
multiple opportunities to put formal language into their own words,
articulating their understanding and misunderstanding, and clari-
fying what they have heard in lectures and read in textbooks. This
process of translating the formal classroom code into expressive
talk and writing takes place in collaboration with peers and trained
tutors who attend the content course with the students.

Like the Hostos model, the program developed at Macalester
pairs an ESL course and a regular introductory content course,
Human Geography, with the language teacher attending the content course along with the students and reading course material.
The ESL teacher meets with the nonnative members of the content course to work on listening comprehension, vocabulary development, critical reading, note-taking, library work, writing, and
discussion of concepts and vocabulary introduced in lectures and
readings. The language course not only facilitates student learning
in Human Geography but also provides support and orientation in

using language to learn in future college courses.

Linking content and language is one solution for offering ESL instruction that moves beyond remediation in response to the linguistic, social, cultural, and intellectual demands made by college courses on nonnative students. Perhaps the most important message of this volume is that improving ESL college instruction means improving the communication among all members of the academic community— native students, nonnative students, content faculty, language faculty, administrators, and counselors. And, we must advocate full membership of our students in this community.

Sarah Benesch
College of Staten Island
City University of New York

References

Hartwell, P. (1985). Grammar, grammars, and the teaching of grammar. *College English*, *47*, 105-127.

Krashen, S. D. (1985). *Inquiries & insights, second language teaching, immersion & bilingual education literacy*. Hayward, CA: Alemany.

Morley, J. (1987). *Current directions in teaching English to speakers of other languages: A state-of-the-art synopsis. TESOL Newsletter*, *21*, 16-20.

✳ Raimes, A. (1985). What unskilled ESL students do as they write: A classroom study of composing. *TESOL Quarterly*, *19*, 229-258.

✳ Rose, M. (1985). The language of exclusion: Writing instruction at the university. *College English*, *47*, 341-359.

Widdowson, H. G. (1978). *Teaching language as communication*. Oxford: Oxford University.

✳ Zamel, V. (1983). The composing processes of advanced ESL students: Six case studies. *TESOL Quarterly*, *17*, 165-187.

✳ Zamel, V. (1982). Writing: The process of discovering meaning. *TESOL Quarterly*, *16*, 195-210.

Using Feedback from ESL Students to Enhance Their Success in College

Trudy Smoke

Hunter College, City University of New York

Abstract

This study uses transcripts and the results of questionnaires sent to 198 ESL students matriculated in a 4-year CUNY college who completed ESL writing courses. Its purpose is to assess students' perceptions and experiences in order to make informed changes in the ESL program. Students perceived a need for a broader academic base in their course work. Although most felt that their language skills had improved because of ESL courses, many did not feel prepared for the demands of credit-bearing content courses. Students wanted more emphasis placed on the skills of reading textbooks, taking notes, and writing research papers. This paper advocates combining content area and language courses around specific academic disciplines to provide students with the skills needed for success in college. The study also suggests that colleges should devote more immediate attention to the problems of the multiple repeater.

Using Feedback from ESL Students to Enhance Their Success in College

ESL teachers remember the hopeful faces of students they helped guide through developmental ESL courses. When these teachers stop to ask former students how they are doing in content courses, too often the response is a shrug or a frown. These ESL students are struggling against enormous odds and in all too many cases are not succeeding in the American college system. As their teachers, many of us ask ourselves what more we can offer these students to make their college experience more rewarding. To this end, the author began a research project to determine how 198 ESL students in a 4-year CUNY college perceived their language learning experiences, anticipating that these perceptions would be useful in making informed changes in ESL offerings.

Background

Cummins (1984) presents evidence that bilingual students have to go beyond conversational fluency to succeed in school; they have to develop the cognitive and academic skills required for learning academic subject matter. Research has been done in several intensive programs which corroborates Cummins' findings.

Christison and Krahnke (1986) conducted open-ended interviews with 80 nonnative English speakers studying in intensive English programs in U.S. colleges and universities. The interviewers found that although students supported the design of most intensive programs, they wanted more interactive instruction. They also asked for more emphasis on the receptive skills of reading and listening over the productive skills of speaking and writing.

Ostler (1980) surveyed 131 advanced ESL students (96 undergraduate and 35 graduate) to determine whether or not the American Language Institute, University of Southern California, was meeting its students' needs. Students requested more preparation in reading texts and taking notes in class. Undergraduates indicated a greater need for the skills of taking multiple choice exams, writing laboratory reports, and reading and making graphs and charts. All students needed help reading academic papers and journals and writing research papers.

The 711 students surveyed by Yorio (1983) in the academic intensive program at the University of Toronto supported most of the learning activities used in that program but did not find translation and memorization of vocabulary to be helpful.

The present study is unlike those cited which deal with students in intensive programs. This research involves nonnative English speakers matriculated in a 4-year CUNY college who have taken credit-bearing courses along with developmental reading and ESL writing courses. It is similar to the cited studies in that the experiences and perceptions of ESL students have proven valuable.

Method

The author randomly selected 198 ESL students who had completed developmental writing between 1980 and 1985. Each student's transcript was reviewed in the fall of 1986. A questionnaire was mailed (see Appendix) or given to students as a personal interview. There have been 62 (31%) responses thus far. Follow-up calls were made and questionnaire interviews were conducted with 14 of the students who were available in the college. The questionnaire will be sent a second time to students who have still not responded.

Findings

Transcripts

Ninety-eight of the original students were still in attendance at the college. A review of the transcripts of the 198 students showed that students who had taken developmental writing more than four times generally had dropped out of college altogether. Of the 98 still in attendance, 44 (46%) had completed freshman composition, ENG 120. Thirty-four students had not passed ENG 120, and 20 students had not yet registered for the course. Of these, several had not registered for freshman composition or any other writing course for more than four semesters.

The ESL students in this study registered for and completed survey courses such as Anthropology 101 and Psychology 101 that do not require research papers and, in general, do not have any writing requirement. The students often elected to take a *Pass* or *Fail* grade in these survey courses rather than the letter grade. Many of these students registered for advanced courses and then withdrew from them during the semester. Even though the students surveyed had been in college more than 2 years, most of them had not yet taken a course in their declared major. Students had most often taken a series of developmental courses in reading, writing, mathematics, and orientation. In addition to these courses, ESL students registered for and completed courses in math and science and in their own first language or a new language more often than in any other area.

Questionnaire

The questionnaire asked students if they felt their English skills had improved as a result of ESL courses; 97% believed they had. Yet when asked if they had felt prepared for college courses when they completed remediation, only 18% said yes. Fifty-seven percent responded that they were "somewhat" prepared and 25% responded that they were not prepared.

When asked what course they would add to the present ESL sequence, 27% responded a pronunciation course, 23% a speech course, and 24% a research paper course.

One question asked respondents to check as many items as were applicable to describe difficulties that they were having in courses that followed the developmental sequence. Ninety-two percent of the students checked "understanding how to read and study from textbooks"; 87% checked "writing research papers"; 81% marked "talking to the professors"; 74% had difficulty "taking notes from lecture classes"; and 71% had problems "answering exam questions."

Another question asked students how they reacted when a research paper was required in a class. Fifty-six percent said they felt nervous, and 37% revealed that they would drop the course. During the interviews, several students said they had never written a research paper and had dropped any course requiring one. Some students revealed that they had had no writing requirement since completing developmental ESL writing courses. "I think I forgot how to write," said one of the students, who was a semester away from graduation.

The questionnaire also asked students who had dropped out of college why they had made this decision. Thirty-eight percent cited "financial reasons," and 26% transferred to another school. Of those, most students went to professional schools—three to nursing schools, one to photography school, one to cosmetology school, and two to computer schools.

Implications

Only 98 students of the original 198 stayed in school, and only 4 of the 100 who left had been graduated. Others sought jobs for financial security; some enrolled in professional schools hoping to have a job in a short time. Still others returned to their home countries.

Such loss does not mean that the college program was a failure; students' language skills had improved. Still we must ask ourselves how we can better serve the ESL population. In questionnaires and interviews, students expressed a need for better preparation to meet the demands and expectations college has for its native and nonnative speakers of English. They expressed a need to blend with the academic community more rapidly. Academia should experiment with strategies to fulfill these needs.

The findings of this study indicate that early intervention is necessary if ESL students are to progress and ultimately succeed in college. Multiple repeaters seemed doomed to drop out of college if some outreach program is not instituted as soon as they have failed one time. Repeating courses over and over again seems to be counterproductive because repeater students are often subjected to the same methods, assignments, and even essay questions semester after semester. One way to better serve these students is to offer combined content area-language courses such as those described by Benesch, Brinton and Snow, and Guyer and Petersen. In this way, students will be involved in a learning experience that will prepare them for mainstream college courses.

Students in such classes will not write essays or read texts in a vacuum. They will not mechanically memorize vocabulary, a process that the 711 students surveyed by Yorio (1983) found to be ineffective. Instead, they will learn vocabulary related to a subject and used frequently in a real academic context. Moreover, the subject matter will have some obvious carry-over to the students' other courses. Students will not have to leave college to attend professional schools to attain success and a job quickly. This experience may motivate them to study and to remain in college.

Some other intervention techniques used for the multiple repeater students include the distribution of profiles to inform teachers of their students' backgrounds and college experiences, the availability of special repeater sections, one-to-one workshops with teachers, and summer intensive programs. In addition, content area discussion groups designed for ESL students and tutors, such as Hirsch's tutoring program, help ESL students to learn and to understand new material as well as to develop the abstracting skills necessary for academic success.

Twenty-seven of the 44 students who passed freshman composition had taken it immediately after completing developmental writing. Thus the time lapse between completion of developmental writing courses and the taking of freshman composition is significant. ESL students should be counseled to take freshman composition immediately upon completion of the developmental writing and reading sequence.

The author found that many students chose courses which required little or no writing. Students stated that although they had completed developmental writing and reading courses, they still did not feel ready to write research papers. If students do not register for freshman composition or if they avoid courses requiring writing, more must be done to encourage students' continuing language development.

One way our colleagues could support efforts to better prepare ESL students would be to require some type of writing in every class. Students need not be required to write research papers; instead they could prepare learning journals, lab reports, or text summaries, to be graded not for mechanics, but for content. These forms of writing place writing in a real context and help students realize that writing is an important skill for all disciplines. Teachers who discern special problems can further aid students by suggesting tutorial assistance.

Students who responded to the questionnaire by stating that they want pronunciation and speech courses seem to be asking for more participation in college. They want to be able to ask or answer questions in front of native-speaking counterparts and feel comfortable in the classroom. Hirsch's tutoring program and other such programs in which ESL students talk about what they are learning respond effectively to this need.

Students also indicated their desire to be better provided with the requisite skills to read a textbook, take notes, and write papers. These skills are necessary to function in mainstream college classes. Combining content area-language courses effectively teaches these skills to ESL classes in which students often have very diverse backgrounds. The combined course creates a common background knowledge, and concepts become more accessible and useful.

Conclusions

Mohan (1986) stated, "A majority of second language learners do not learn language for its own sake. They learn because they must learn subject matter through the medium of the second language. They must use the second language to learn" (p. 1). Although we may be somewhat successful preparing our students to communicate better, we may not be doing enough to address their basic academic concerns. Students need to feel that they have the language competence to function in the classroom and in the library. Colleges can provide this competence with bridge or combined content area-language courses to teach receptive skills, such as reading a textbook or a piece of literature and listening to a lecture and productive skills, such as are involved in making oral presentations, taking notes, using the library, and writing research papers. These minimum competencies are required of all college students and are not taught in most developmental programs.

Although this paper advocates combining content area and language courses, not all schools can implement the suggestion, as it involves investments of time and money that may not be immediately available. But some intermediate steps can introduce the ESL student to the larger academic community. Within the context of developmental ESL classes, teachers can create units of study centered around a particular academic discipline having a consistent vocabulary. These might include reading from journalistic sources, textbooks, and literature, but they should all concern the same subject matter and, as much as possible, be interesting and important to the entire class. In this way, the content provides the context for learning.

Using the subject framework selected by the class, the teacher can guide the students in using the library to write brief, relevant research papers and in giving oral presentations which may be audio- and/or videotaped. Individual or small-group conferences can be centered around these written and spoken presentations with students getting support, guidance, and feedback as quickly as possible. As students become more familiar with the terminology of a particular discipline, they may benefit from a variety of activities. A guest speaker may be invited to class or a colleague's taped lecture can be played in class. Students will take notes, and then as a group, students can discuss the choices made in their note-taking process. Class discussions based on the academic context should be encouraged and, if possible, other ESL students or native speakers should be invited to participate or respond.

Once connections are made between departments in the college, it becomes easier to set up pilot combined content area-language courses. Even if the technique is tried with only one class for one semester, colleagues will realize that combining their teaching with the language course makes their job more satisfying because students' oral and written work will improve. Students will comprehend lectures and participate in class discussions more freely, once they understand vocabulary and basic concepts in the discipline. The process of creating such combined courses may proceed slowly, but it is important to pursue them to facilitate ESL students' development.

This preliminary study has reinforced the concept that students can directly or indirectly offer valuable information about their language learning experience. Perhaps this will encourage more detailed and rigorous investigations into student feedback, yielding data that may improve ESL students' experiences in higher education. It is also hoped that more colleges will create connections between language and content area courses. Students need to see that language skills develop within meaningful contexts, and colleges can best provide for ESL students by making this experience available.

References

Christison, M. A., Krahnke, K. J. (1986). Student perceptions of academic language study. *TESOL Quarterly, 20,* 61-78.

Cummins, J. (1984). *Bilingualism and special education.* San Diego: College Hill.

Mohan, B. A. (1986). Language and content learning: Finding common ground. *ERIC/CLL News Bulletin, 9,* 1,8-9.

Ostler, S. E. (1980). Survey of academic needs for advanced ESL. *TESOL Quarterly, 14,* 489-502.

Yorio, C. A. (1983, October). The use of student surveys in second language programming. Paper presented at the 2nd Rocky Mountain Regional TESOL Conference, Salt Lake City, UT.

Appendix

Questionnaire

Name _____

Address _____ Male ____ Female ____

_____ Telephone ____

Place of birth _____ Date of birth

Please answer the following questions:
1. How many years have you lived in the United States? _____
2. How old were you when you came to the United States? _____
3. When you are at home with your family do you speak English?
   ___ Often ___ Sometimes ___ Never
4. Do you have a job? ___ Yes ___ No
   ___ Full-time ___ Part-time

5. When you are at work do you speak English?
___ Often ___ Sometimes ___ Never
6. Did you study English in your native country?
___ Yes ___ No
For how long? _____ How many hours per week? _____
7. Were you in special ESL classes in high school in the United States? ___ Yes ___ No
8. Do you feel your English skills improved as a result of your college ESL courses? ___ Yes ___ No
9. If you could have dropped a class from your ESL program, what class would you have dropped? _____
10. If you could have added a class to your ESL program, what class would you have added? _____
11. When you completed remediation were you prepared for college courses? ___ Yes ___ No ___ Somewhat prepared
12. What could your ESL classes have done to better prepare you for college work? _____
(If you need more space, use the back of the page.)
13. The biggest problems in classes after remediation were: (Check as many as are true for you.)
___ understanding the professor
___ understanding how to read and study from textbooks
___ taking notes from lecture classes
___ writing research papers
___ using the library
___ none of the above
___ talking to other students in class
___ talking to the professors
___ asking questions in the class
___ answering exam questions
___ typing
14. The easiest part of taking classes after you completed remediation were:
___ understanding the professor
___ understanding how to read and study from textbooks
___ taking notes from lecture classes
___ writing research papers
___ using the library
___ none of the above
___ talking to other students in class
___ talking to the professors
___ asking questions in the class
___ answering exam questions
___ typing
15. When you find that a research paper is required in a class, do you feel: ___ confident ___ nervous ___ that you should drop the course.

16. What do you think is most important to teachers when they grade your work? ____ grammar ____ ideas ____ spelling ____ neatness ____ vocabulary
17. If you did not take freshman composition immediately after you finished remediation, was it because:
    ___ there were no available sections
    ___ you felt like you needed a break
18. If you did not pass freshman composition the first time you took it, was it because of:
    ___ the research paper   ___ the final exam
    ___ the classwork   ___ the teacher
19. Do you have any good friends with whom you speak only English?
    ___ many ___ a few ___ one ___ none
20. If you are no longer a student in the college, did you leave because of: (Check the most important reason for you.)
    ___ graduation   ___ financial need
    ___ family problems   ___ school difficulties
    ___ transfer to another school
    (If so, which school did you transfer to?) _____

Thank you for your help in answering this questionnaire. If you would like to add anything else about your experience learning English, please write in the space below.

c. 1986
T. Smoke

About the Author

Trudy Smoke coordinates ESL in the Department of Academic Skills at Hunter College, CUNY. She is also a doctoral student at New York University and is the author of the ESL text, *A Writer's Workbook*, published by St. Martin's Press.

When There Are No Links Between ESL and Content Courses

Elaine Brooks

Brooklyn College, City University of New York

Abstract

This paper discusses the efforts of the ESL faculty of an urban 4-year college to prepare students in their program for the demands of a core of 10 required academic courses. To determine ways students would need and be expected to use English in core courses, ESL faculty sought out instructors of core courses to learn about syllabi, reading lists, writing assignments, and tests. They intended to revise ESL curricula consequently. One finding of their project was a lack of ongoing communication between core and ESL faculty about academic uses of language and how to help students develop these. ESL seemed to be treated as a service program. To prepare students for other courses, ESL should be integrated more carefully with other disciplines and include more communication with other faculty.

When There Are No Links Between ESL
and Content Courses

> A majority of second language learners do not learn
> language for its own sake. They learn because they must
> learn subject matter through the medium of the second
> language . . . . Accordingly, the integration of language
> learning and content learning is now considered an impor-
> tant question in the field of language research. (Mohan,
> 1986, p. 1)

In any academic program attempting to facilitate students'
development in English, it is important to consider whom the
program is intended to serve, what the structure of the program
implies about its purpose, and what types of courses students will
enter outside the program. This can not be done well in isolation;
ESL faculty need to be in contact with non-ESL colleagues and be
knowledgeable about what is done in their courses.

Since 1980 a major concern of the ESL faculty at Brooklyn
College, a unit of the City University of New York, has been to
understand the demands of the college's core curriculum, a group
of 10 courses required for graduation (see Appendix). This paper
will discuss a project carried out by the ESL faculty to determine
ways in which students would need and be expected to use English in
such courses. Unlike other papers in the volume, this paper does
not discuss a program or technique which links ESL and content
courses; rather, it reflects on the way one program functions when
such links are lacking.

The ESL Program: Its Population, Purpose, and Structure

The English-as-a-Second-Language Program at Brooklyn College
is a component of the Department of Educational Services, serv-
ing matriculated students pursuing an undergraduate degree. These
students have not yet passed the university skills assessments tests
in reading or writing. Some have passed one of the tests; others
have failed both. The ESL Program's classes are "taught with the
intention of aiding the L2 students' achievement in content
classes . . ." (Mohan, 1979, p. 179).

To accommodate students coming into this program at varying

levels of ability, the program offers five levels of ESL writing courses, four of reading, and two of speech. Students are placed into these courses according to scores they receive at entry on assessment tests, similar to placement testing done in other colleges. The program is flexible: if students score higher in writing than reading, they are placed into the appropriate level for each; or, if students pass one test but not the other, they take whichever course is needed. Students do not have to take each level or type of course, but the courses are available when needed. The program accommodates students whose writing, reading, and speaking abilities vary.

The College's Core Curriculum

Similar to that of other colleges across the country, the Brooklyn College Core is meant to provide students with a common base and confirm "the importance of humanistic and liberal undergraduate studies" (Van Solkema, 1983, p. 2). Although the 10 courses were designed to complement each other, much of the integration of material is currently left to the individual student. The designers of these core courses hoped to foster integration by requiring writing, a way of learning, in every course; there is also supposed to be coordination with and reinforcement of the freshman writing courses (English I and II). Students benefit further from annual college-wide faculty seminars that shape the evolution of and evaluate these courses within the total curriculum.

How do core planners see their relation to basic skills and ESL faculty and students? Although every committee planning the core included a member of the Educational Services Department to discuss skills and accessibility, planners generally assume students will have passed the assessment tests *before* beginning core classes. When considering how students will plan their programs, allowing for the core requirement, faculty assume that all students will complete *all* core courses by the end of the sixth term or 96 credits, *except* for ESL students "who are given additional flexibility in the sequence and number of core courses to be taken in a term" (Van Solkema, 1983, p. 21).

The assumption that students will already have acquired basic reading and writing skills (as measured by assessment tests) before entering core classes creates problems for both faculty and students. In actuality, ESL students often take core and ESL courses concurrently, depending on which assessment tests they have passed. Furthermore, minimum competency, as measured by such tests, may not be sufficient; it permits students to enter freshman composition and other courses but may not get them through (Brooks, 1987).

Ongoing discussion or collaboration between core and ESL faculty, in addition to informal or personal initiatives, would further clarify how language development and other areas of learning overlap and develop for both native and nonnative users of English. Although faculty from the ESL Program and the Department of Educational Services are invited to college-wide faculty core seminars, it is difficult to gauge how much influence such faculty may have. Unfortunately, there has been little formal or structured opportunity for core teachers to "profit from observing the way communication succeeds . . . in classes taught by experienced ESL teachers" (Mohan, 1979, p. 176). Nonetheless, ESL faculty at the college have made efforts to inform themselves about the content and requirements of the core curriculum and to revise their curriculum and procedures with nonnative students. One such undertaking influenced ESL course syllabi.

The Project

Inspired by the introduction of the core curriculum, ESL faculty members began to investigate the content and demands of these courses. In spring, 1982, Professors Bains, Brooks, and Fox wrote a proposal and began gathering data to help them assess and improve ESL students' linguistic ability to cope with the reading and writing assignments and exams in the new curriculum. They proposed a 3-year plan to develop collaboration between language and content teachers as follows. During the first year, ESL faculty would discuss with core faculty the latter's expectations of students, investigate students' academic backgrounds, and test groups of ESL and non-ESL students (to determine what students took from readings or to evaluate their writing) and compare results. In the second year, ESL faculty would develop materials and methods for tutoring students in "skills areas." During the third year, non-ESL faculty would attend seminars on working effectively with ESL students (Bains, Brooks, & Fox, 1982). The three professors hoped this proposal could lead to improved ESL course curricula, more effective tutoring facilities, and more sensitized non-ESL faculty.

One assumption of the proposal was that all entering college students lack skills (Maeroff, 1981). The ESL Program ought to identify what skills students need in core courses and prepare students, particularly those lacking certain academic skills in addition to English language development. Some of the needs identified in this proposal were the ability to comprehend lectures and readings and take notes from each, skim texts for main ideas and supporting points, use a dictionary and the library, fulfill reading and writing assignments, and study for and take exams.

The investigators examined the types of reading and writing assignments and tests given in core courses for the following information: how much reading or writing is assigned, and how it is handled; where and why would students' comprehension of material break down; and what kind of activities take place, i.e., pre- or postreading and writing. They also interviewed instructors about their expectations and plans for evaluation as well as about the weight given to content versus form in students' work. They planned to interview students to discover how they prepared for assignments and tests and to identify what difficulties they experienced with each. They collected core course syllabi, reading lists, writing assignments, and copies of exams. They talked with instructors of courses and sat in on classes. The investigators' purpose was to revise *ESL* curricula, tests, and materials as a result of their efforts: "ESL faculty can determine *exactly* [italics added] what the academic needs of their students are if they are allowed to observe and study subject area courses" (Bains, et al., 1982, p. 17).

Discussion

Although only the initial phase of the proposal has been completed, the information gathered has led to concrete results. Responses from core faculty varied. Some instructors were helpful, providing handouts about course reading lists and writing assignments, while others were discomforted by the attention, perhaps concerned that their teaching was being evaluated. Overall, colleagues in other departments appeared enthusiastic about improving their ability to reach students and increasing students' opportunities to learn in core courses and throughout their college careers. Maintaining and enlarging the possibilities for both ESL and non-ESL faculties to share information about how to facilitate learning is important; neither group can do its job realistically or well without recognizing the links between content and language.

Discussions among ESL faculty led to revisions and updates of various ESL course syllabi. Initial contacts were made with colleagues in other departments. A textbook was published (Fox, 1986) as an attempt to integrate core content and language teaching. Readings for the ESL program are now drawn from a wider variety of disciplines, especially at the advanced levels where ESL students are already likely to be in one or more core courses. There are greater efforts to integrate reading and writing assignments, particularly responses to short essay questions which students face on exams in other courses. ESL faculty have also emphasized abilities such as critical thinking, summary, and synthesis which students will be expected to demonstrate in extensive writing assignments in core classes.

Although the proposal recognized that there were demands on students greater than simply passing minimal competency tests, the investigators seemed to *assume* that the ESL program helps students cope with only the *linguistic* demands of college courses. As Mohan (1979) might put it, the program's purpose is language teaching to prepare for or facilitate students' achievement in content courses. In contrast to their point of view, Mohan (1979) "shows how widely accepted definitions of language teaching are inadequate, failing to take acccount of overlap with content teaching and the teaching of cognitive skills" (p. 171). The investigators' proposal and plans did not concern language alone. They were going to examine the content and cognitive tasks as well as the linguistic requirements of core courses.

The ESL faculty assumed they could get information from core course colleagues or vice versa. The idea of such an exchange between "language" and "content" teachers without mutual consideration of the connections between language and content now seems naive and simplistic. A more useful addition to the proposal (with hindsight) might have been a collaboration between language and core faculties to structure courses or develop curricula, much as writing instructors have been used as resources wherever writing-across-the-curriculum has been instituted.

What assumptions do core faculty make? Their courses are meant to be introductory, to prepare a foundation for students to build upon. What do the faculty assume *all* students will already know or be able to do when entering such courses? The ESL faculty's proposal suggested that ESL and non-ESL teachers would discuss how to make lectures, reading and writing assignments, and tests more accessible to *ESL* students, with *ESL* faculty *guiding* core faculty in techniques. There was no strong suggestion of collaboration, nor was there any suggestion that collaboration might benefit native students or ESL faculty as well. Two projects were initiated recently by core faculty members—peer-tutoring and a mentoring program—for students who passed the assessment tests but whose high school records indicate they may be at risk in terms of retention. There could be more continuous and fruitful sharing of information between ESL and core faculty to more accurately reflect the overlap of their respective fields.

Suggestions

In discussing L2 teaching for content teaching and the assumption that language teaching, content teaching, and thinking activities are inseparable and mutually dependent, Mohan (1979) also points out the following:

> This discussion should go beyond the case where a general basic ESL course teaches a student some English with the result that student can make some sense of any content course he takes later. This is likely to happen to some degree with any language course and requires no particular curriculum planning . . . . The aim should be more general and long term: to see what LT [language teaching] curriculum can help students manage content learning tasks independently. (p. 179)

This paper suggests a need for further research into what is being done and could be done towards understanding the relationships between learning and teaching, language and content. ESL programs are sometimes seen as service courses, meant to prepare students for other courses. These programs should be integrated more carefully with other disciplines and include more communication with other faculties to fulfill their function. When ESL instructors try to integrate language and content teaching, we ought to be aware of assumptions made in our classrooms and programs—about students, the role of faculty, courses students are or will be taking, and our definitions of terms such as *content* and *language*. Similarly, when *language teaching* and *content teaching* are discussed separately, what do they we think is the content of the language class? And how do we feel language influences the teaching of content?

The Core Curriculum of Brooklyn College, the academic setting described in this paper, involves the participation of specialists from different disciplines in planning, executing, and evaluating its courses; it could allow for still greater participation and input of ESL and developmental faculty and students. The ESL faculty's efforts take place mainly within its own program. What does the fact that these two groups of faculty (ESL and core) appear to function separately imply about their assumptions in relation to how they plan courses, see each other, and conceive the relationships between learning and teaching, language and content? Furthermore, what does this separation indicate to students? Working with other ESL faculty and more consistently with non-ESL faculty will enable instructors to determine how to best achieve the goals of sharing skills and helping students develop effectively. There are a few ways links might be developed. ESL faculty can help non-ESL colleagues understand the purpose and structure of the ESL program so they will better understand students' development, be able to refer students, or make use of ESL resources. Ongoing, active ESL participation in college-wide curriculum development could ensure mutual understanding of the links between language and content for all students, native and nonnative.

Because minimum competency is often not enough to prepare students to function well in courses, and faculty are sometimes unaware of ESL students in larger classes, ongoing support services and resources for students, such as peer- or writing-tutors with some ESL training, should be available. (See the Smoke and Hirsch papers in this volume.) When ESL faculty must work alone, they can inform themselves about the content and requirements of other courses in shaping their own. They should try to build communication with other faculty (and administrators), perhaps creating joint research projects to assess and improve students' linguistic preparedness or to consider the overlap between teaching content and cognitive skills, for greater understanding of their mutual task.

References

Bains, G., Brooks, E., & Fox, L. (1982). *Preparing ESL students for core curriculum courses.* Unpublished research proposal, Brooklyn College, CUNY, Brooklyn, NY.

Brooks, E. (1988). *Follow-through: An update of a study of the composing processes of 'unskilled' college writers.* (Practical Research II: Studies in ESL for Underprepared College Students.) The City University of New York, Office of Special Programs.

Fox, L. (1986). *Gateway: A cross-curricular reading and writing book.* San Diego: Harcourt Brace Jovanovich.

Maeroff, G. I. (1981, March 31). CUNY leads in remedial program. *New York Times,* C2.

Mohan, B. (1979). Relating language teaching and content teaching. *TESOL Quarterly, 13,* 171-181.

Mohan, B. (1986). Language and content learning: Finding common ground. *ERIC/ Clearinghouse on Languages and Linguistic News Bulletin, 9,* 1.

Van Solkema, S., Fried, V., Lifshitz, B., Shapiro, G., Shepetin, L., Trefousse, H., & Wolfe, E. (1983). *The introduction to the core curriculm.* New York: Brooklyn College.

Appendix

The Core Curriculum: An Overview

First Tier

Core Studies 1	Classical Origins of Western Culture
Core Studies 2	Introduction to Art (2.1)
	Introduction to Music (2.2)
Core Studies 3	People, Power, and Politics
Core Studies 4	The Shaping of the Modern World
Core Studies 5	Introduction to Mathematical Reasoning and Computer Programming

Second Tier

Core Studies 6	Landmarks of Literature
Core Studies 7	Science in Modern Life I: Chemistry (7.1) and Physics (7.2)
Core Studies 8	Science in Modern Life II: Biology (8.1) and Geology (8.2)
Core Studies 9	Studies in African, Asian, and Latin American cultures
Core Studies 10	Knowledge, Existence, and Values

Foreign language study through Level 3 or equivalent proficiency

About the Author

Elaine Brooks is Assistant Professor of English, Brooklyn College, City University of New York. She has an MA in TESOL (Teachers College, Columbia), and a PhD in Applied Linguistics (New York University). Her dissertation and current research focus on the composing processes of ESL college writers. In 1986-1987, Dr. Brooks co-coordinated the ESL program at Brooklyn College. She is currently a member of the Brooklyn College Committee on Undergraduate Curriculum and Degree Requirements.

The Adjunct Model of Language Instruction: An Ideal EAP Framework

Marguerite Ann Snow

Donna M. Brinton

University of California, Los Angeles

Abstract

This paper describes the adjunct model of language instruction—an instructional model in which English/ESL courses are linked with content courses to better integrate the reading, writing, and study skills required for academic success at the university. The paper provides a rationale for the adjunct model based on three other movements in language teaching and describes key features of the adjunct program implemented at UCLA, including methodology, content-based curriculum development, materials adaptation and development, instructor coordination, and the role of the language instructor. In the final section, strengths of the model are discussed as well as applications of the model to other ESL/EFL settings.

The Adjunct Model of Language Instruction:
An Ideal EAP Framework

Every summer at UCLA, the Freshman Summer Program or FSP, is offered to entering students who have been identified as "high risk" in the admissions process. FSP is a 7-week intensive preparatory program that was established in 1977 to bridge the gap between high school and college. In the view of the UCLA administration, those asked to enroll in FSP have been inadequately prepared in their high school education for the academic rigors of the university environment, particularly with respect to their reading, writing, and study skills. Their potential for academic success is considered to be tenuous.

The primary academic goal of FSP is to "introduce underprepared students to the intellectual and sociobureaucratic demands of the university," to teach them to deal with "increasingly complex exposition on academic topics," and "to dispel the simplified notions of disciplines that many high school students have" (Rose, 1982, p. 8). Equally important goals of FSP are to provide students with the social and recreational needs so important in this transition period, build positive self-images, and ensure emotional stability throughout the program. The former goal is achieved through FSP's academic component; the latter are accomplished through the program's on-campus residential program, academic and personal counseling services, forums and social programs, and tutorial services.

FSP employs the adjunct model of language instruction in which content courses (e.g., Introduction to Psychology, Introductory Political Science) are linked with language courses to better integrate the reading, writing, and study skill requirements of the two disciplines. In the language class, students are tracked into a series of composition courses appropriate to their proficiency level and language background. All students are concurrently enrolled in one of six content courses, with the language and content courses unified by the coordination of the course syllabi. The ultimate academic goal of the program is to equip students with the independent thinking, writing, and study skills required for future academic work.

The rationale for the adjunct model used in FSP is articulated in the theoretical underpinnings of at least three movements in language teaching. The "Language Across the Curriculum" movement (Bullock Report, 1975), which originated in Britain, suggests that effective language teaching must cross over all subject matter domains. The perspective calls for a reciprocal relationship between language and content. Students must be given opportunities to learn to write and learn to read but must also be allowed to write to learn and read to learn in order to fully participate in the educational process.

A rationale for the adjunct model used in FSP can also be found in the English for Special Purposes (ESP) literature. While FSP students' aims might more precisely be labeled as English for Academic Purposes (EAP), the theoretical justification remains the same. Widdowson (1983) notes:

> In ESP we are dealing with students for whom the learning of English is auxiliary to some other professional or academic purpose. It is clearly a means for achieving something else and is not an end in itself. . . . This being so, ESP is (or ought logically to be) integrally linked with areas of activity (academic, vocational, professional) which have already been defined and which represent the learners' aspirations. (pp. 108-109)

Elsewhere, Widdowson (1978) advocates integrating or linking language teaching in the schools with other subjects (e.g., physics, chemistry, biology, map drawing) "as this not only helps ensure the link with reality and the pupils' own experience, but also provides us with the most certain means of teaching language as communication, as use rather than simply as usage" (p. 16).

Thus, integrated courses, or content-based courses as they are often called, represent a curricular innovation in keeping with the current learning-across-the-curriculum movement at the secondary level in American schools (cf. Anderson, Eisenberg, Hooland, Wiener, & Rivera-Kron, 1983) and the extensive work in ESP. Perhaps the most documented model of content-based language instruction is immersion education, in which monolingual children at the elementary and secondary levels receive the majority of the standard school curriculum in the second language. Begun in Montreal in 1965, this model of foreign language teaching has since spread throughout Canada and the United States. The successes of immersion with language majority students have been repeated in a number of different target languages (e.g., French, Spanish, German, Cantonese) and in a variety of ethnolinguistic settings (Rhodes & Schreibstein, 1983).

Although the three movements discussed differ in their implementation of content-based curricula, they share the same basic pedagogical assumption: Successful language learning occurs when students are exposed to content material presented in meaningful, contextualized form, with the focus on acquiring information. Moreover, the approaches represent an effective method of integrating the language curriculum with the academic or occupational interests of the students.

Description of the UCLA Freshman Summer Program

UCLA's FSP provides an excellent example of a content-based instructional program designed to meet the linguistic and academic needs of underprepared students. The curriculum of FSP is based on the adjunct prototype at California State University, Dominguez Hills (Sutton, 1978) and on the research findings of Rose (1980), who examined the kinds of writing required of UCLA undergraduate students in a variety of disciplines. Rose found that the most common written discourse mode required in both assignments and examinations was exposition; specifically, students were being asked to write essays of seriation, classification, summary to synthesis, compare/ contrast, and analysis.

The academic component of FSP consists of various ESL/English composition courses and six content courses — Psychology, Political Science, Geography, Social Science, Computer Science, and Anthropology — introductory courses which undergraduates typically take to fulfill their university breadth requirements (See Figure 1). Students attend 12-14 hours of language classes weekly, while the combined lecture/discussion section format of the content course comprises approximately 8 contact hours per week. Course content in both the language and subject-matter classes parallels that of courses offered during the normal academic year, with minor modifications made to facilitate coordination between the two disciplines.

Student Population

Students admitted to UCLA with low verbal SAT and ACT scores are invited to attend FSP. Acceptance at UCLA is not generally contingent on participation in FSP; however, those initially contacted are encouraged to attend. Approximately 500 students attend the program each summer. Participants consist mostly of low income, ethnic minority, or linguistic minority students. The bulk of the ESL students are Asian immigrants (with the majority

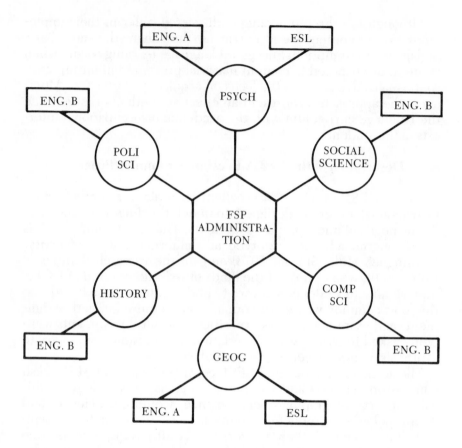

Figure 1: The academic component of the UCLA Freshman Summer Program

being Korean, Chinese, and Vietnamese students) who have completed their secondary education in the United States. For the
purposes of this article, we will address our remarks to our experience working with ESL students in FSP.

The following information is a profile of the academic deficien-
cies of the ESL students enrolled in FSP. In a recent summer,
students enrolled in the lower proficiency level ESL classes had an
average SAT verbal score of 225, while their average math score
was 527. The Sequential Test of Educational Progress (STEP) also
provides evidence of the weak reading skills of the ESL students in

FSP. Their average percentile ranking was .08, i.e., they were collectively lower than the first percentile, thus ranking lower than approximately 99% of entering college freshmen, the population on whom the test was normed (Snow & Brinton, 1984).

Methodology

Assignments in the ESL component of the adjunct program are based almost entirely on material from the content course. A typical first reading activity is a survey of the content course textbook. Students have to answer a series of questions which requires them to use the table of contents, index, references, glossary, etc. Reading strategies such as previewing, scanning, and skimming can be practiced throughout the term using the content course textbook.

In terms of composition skills, a typical lesson on definition from the Psychology adjunct would require students to use their psychology lecture notes on the effects of LSD in a controlled drug experiment to define the important terms. Building from sentence level, the next writing activity might involve a paragraph-length assignment of definition (e.g., a dictation or dictocomp defining hallucinations and delusions). A subsequent composition assignment might require students to read a case study of an LSD experience and, using examples from the case study, to write an extended definition paper on drug-induced psychosis.

Likewise, a grammar lesson on conditionals might capitalize on the psychological concept of stimulus response. Students would practice writing different types of conditional sentences from given cues, demonstrating both understanding of the psychological process and command of the grammatical structure. Given the cues *early weaning* and *dependency and pessimism,* for example, a student might produce a sentence such as "If a mother weans her child too early, the child will grow up to be dependent and pessimistic." In such assignments equal emphasis is placed on the accuracy of both content and structure.

Finally, a major focus of the adjunct class is the development of study skills. The most immediate concern when the term begins is helping students learn how to take good lecture notes through listening strategies and note-taking organization. In addition to giving practice lectures on topics in the content course, language instructors attend the content course lectures. The instructors' notes are then used as model notes for information exchange exercises and class discussion.

Coordination

The adjunct model requires close coordination among staff members of the linked courses (e.g., administrative staff, instructors, tutors, and counselors), to achieve its intent. All instructors attend a series of meetings before the term begins to determine the program's shape and specifics. In these meetings discussion usually focuses on how to best dovetail the English/ESL syllabus with that of the content course, and decisions are made on which discourse mode to focus each week (e.g., definition, compare/contrast). Of particular importance to the English/ESL staff are the criteria by which the content course staff will grade written work, and discussion of this usually centers on how to evaluate structural (especially ESL) and stylistic problems. Finally, both groups discuss complementary assignments and coordination of efforts to improve students' study skills.

Weekly meetings are scheduled to ensure cooperation between the two teams throughout the instructional period. These provide a forum for discussion of the week's evaluation activity (examination or paper assignment) in the content course and of individual student progress and/or problems. When necessary, decisions are made to refer students to tutorial and counseling services. Finally, these meetings allow for continued coordination of program goals so that the same objectives are being reinforced by every instructor with whom the student comes into contact.

Text Selection and Adaptation

Given the highly specific nature of the adjunct language course, issues of text selection and materials preparation are important. One legitimate question concerns the choice of an appropriate content course text: If students have low-level language skills, can they read and comprehend college-level academic texts? Experience has confirmed our opinion that while selecting a simplified text does students a disservice, selecting a convoluted, poorly written text does them an equal disservice, because they will be frustrated in attempts to apply developing reading strategies. The program's goals are to use *authentic* content material and to assist students to grapple with the text by providing them access to improved strategies for reading and studying. In theory, the answer lies in choosing a challenging, well-written content text with adequate visuals, study guides, glosses, and other ancillary materials. In reality, the choice of the content text is often not the prerogative of the language instructor, who may well have to cope with the predetermined choice of the content course instructor.

A second question which arises is whether or not commercial ESL materials are usable in adjunct ESL instruction, and if so, to what extent do they need to be adapted? Our experience argues for the use of ESL texts as references for both teachers and students. We rely heavily on commercial ESL texts for treatment of the English article system or transitional expressions of comparison/contrast, for example. We feel, however, that it is imperative to supplement commercial texts with teacher-developed materials relating directly to the content course materials, and much of our time is devoted to tasks such as preparing reading guides, writing sentence-combining exercises based on the content area material, devising sample essay questions, and providing model answers.

The Role of ESL Instructors

The underlying philosophy of the adjunct model requires that language instructors assume a dual responsibility. Their primary purpose is to provide instruction that will promote English language development. Because this is done through the medium of content material, the language instructor must also be familiar with this material. Thus, for the English/ESL instructor to be maximally effective, a substantial amount of time must be devoted to:

1. Learning the material of the content course;
2. Developing language teaching materials based on the content; and
3. Providing feedback on both the linguistic aspects of the students' work and (to a lesser degree) the quality of the content.

Even with the emphasis placed on content course material, the English/ESL instructor still has to face the responsibility of meeting specified objectives of the language course. Instructors in an adjunct program, therefore, may have to juggle the demands of the standard language syllabus with constraints placed on it by the adjunct hookup and may have to resolve possible disparities between the two. Clearly, there are limitations to the dual responsibilities of the language teacher. Though the adjunct model by definition requires English/ ESL instructors to function within certain guidelines, these instructors are in no way meant to supersede the content course teaching staff. Rather, the two teams must work in tandem.

Strengths of the Adjunct Model

Instructor Evaluation

From our point of view as instructors, the adjunct model offers multiple strengths. The most immediately evident of these is the efficacy of its pedagogical framework in an academic setting. The model offers other attractive features, including the student population itself, which is more homogeneous and more uniformly motivated than the traditional ESL class. By expanding the dynamics of teaching to include general academic preparation as well as language instruction, the model offers ESL teachers a more broadly defined domain of teaching and the opportunity to be truly involved in preparing students for university study. Thus, the essence of the adjunct model's appeal to instructors involves the following: the rewards of working within a sound pedagogical framework, the challenge of rising to the responsibility for materials development and coordination, the insights gained by direct involvement with academic demands placed on students, and the opportunity to share in the students' successes and failures in content courses.

Student Evaluations

Questionnaires are administered at the end of each session asking students to rate the overall effectiveness of FSP and the value of its individual components. (A copy of the questionnaire appears in the Appendix.) In general, both native English students and ESL students consistently rate FSP very highly. Reported in Table 1 are the selected student responses from a recent summer to key items from Part A of the questionnaire on the language component. The table gives student ratings broken down by English and ESL proficiency levels.

From these responses we see strong support for teacher convictions about the merits of the adjunct model: An overwhelming 82.2% of all students agreed that they were better writers as a result of FSP; likewise, they indicated that the FSP language component had helped them read their content course texts and complete content course writing assignments more effectively (91.4% and 75.6%, respectively). Interestingly, the lower proficiency ESL 33B/English A students gave higher ratings on items 2-3 than did the rest of the students. This level effect most likely reflects an interaction between the former groups' intensified awareness of their language needs and the heavy writing and reading demands placed on them by the program. Similarly, in assessing their

Table 1: *Selected Student Ratings of Language Component—Part A*

		n	% Agree	% No Opinion	% Disagree	% No Answer
Item #1: I am a better writer then when I entered FSP	ESL 33B	33	75.8	9.1	15.2	0.00
	ESL 33C	53	71.7	13.2	15.1	0.00
	ENG A	108	92.6	6.5	.9	0.00
	ENG 1	220	88.6	8.6	2.7	0.00
	ALL FSP	414	82.2	9.4	8.5	0.00
Item #2: This course helped me to write better papers for my breadth course	ESL 33B	33	97.0	3.0	0.00	0.00
	ESL 33C	53	88.7	9.4	1.9	0.00
	ENG A	108	90.8	6.5	1.9	0.9
	ENG 1	220	89.1	8.6	1.4	0.9
	ALL FSP	414	91.4	7.0	1.3	0.5
Item #3: This course helped me to read my breadth course text more effectively	ESL 33B	33	81.9	18.2	0.00	0.00
	ESL 33C	53	75.5	20.8	3.8	0.00
	ENG A	108	76.9	14.8	7.4	0.9
	ENG 1	220	68.2	22.7	9.1	0.00
	ALL FSP	414	75.6	19.1	5.1	0.2

overall writing improvement (item 1), the two ESL groups were more cautious in their ratings—a fact which may be attributed to their discouragement over the large number of residual structural errors.

Part B of the questionnaire asked students to rate discrete activities in the language component, and we were again encouraged to find concurrence with our general evaluation of the activities. Table 2 compares ESL 33B (n = 33) student responses to those of all other FSP participants on this section of the questionnaire (n = 381).

Table 2 shows that despite differences in the student populations polled (i.e., level differences, native vs. nonnative speaker participants, etc.), the 33B rankings for class activity usefulness correlate highly with those obtained for all other FSP students polled (Spearman rho = .9, p > .01). Both groups indicated written comments on papers, grammar presentations and exercises, and in-class writing as the three most useful categories. Given the strong emphasis in the content course on writing correct, organized prose, this came as no surprise to us: Students obviously valued the strong integration between the language class and the content course writing assignment.

We were somewhat disappointed at the relatively low ranking of study skills and reading—a component of the course which we perceived as an extremely high priority. We suspect that this relatively low ranking for an activity to which we devoted a weekly average of 4-5 class hours can be explained by students' overestimation of their reading skills coupled with a lack of awareness of how crucial good study habits are at the university. Finally, we were surprised at the low rankings of peer editing, student presen-

Table 2: *Selected Student Ratings of Language Component—Part B*

		Rank*	% Helpful	% So-So	% Not Helpful	% No Answer**
Written Comments	ESL 33B	1	97.0	0.00	0.00	3.0
on Papers	ALL FSP	1	94.5	2.3	0.00	3.2
Grammar Lectures	ESL 33B	2	93.9	1.5	1.5	3.0
and Exercises	ALL FSP	3	87.3	7.3	1.5	4.0
In-Class	ESL 33B	3	93.9	0.00	3.0	3.0
Writing	ALL FSP	2	89.2	5.5	1.3	4.0
Class	ESL 33B	4	90.9	9.1	0.00	0.00
Discussion	ALL FSP	4	85.0	12.4	0.5	2.1
Take-Home	ESL 33B	5	90.9	6.1	0.00	3.0
Writing	ALL FSP	8	74.9	9.3	1.5	14.3
Prewriting and	ESL 33B	6	87.9	6.1	3.0	3.0
Planning	ALL FSP	5	83.8	6.4	1.3	8.5
Study Skills	ESL 33B	7	84.9	12.1	3.0	0.00
and Reading	ALL FSP	7	78.3	13.3	2.7	5.7
Revising	ESL 33B	8	72.7	12.1	3.0	12.1
	ALL FSP	6	79.0	8.8	1.1	11.1
Small Peer	ESL 33B	9	60.6	27.3	6.1	6.1
Edit Groups	ALL FSP	10	56.7	22.6	7.4	13.3
Student	ESL 33B	10	54.5	39.4	0.00	6.1
Presentations	ALL FSP	11	45.5	32.2	4.4	17.9
Teacher	ESL 33B	11	45.5	18.2	3.0	33.3
Conferences	ALL FSP	9	61.4	9.9	1.5	27.3

*Spearman rho = .9, p > .01
**Combines "No answer" and "Didn't Reply" categories

tations, and teacher conferences. Quite possibly, our students, straight out of the high school system, were unaccustomed to all three of these or (in the case of teacher consultation) were reluctant to take advantage of them and thus did not value them as highly as more traditional classroom activities.

Perhaps the most gratifying evidence for the adjunct model comes out of Part C of the evaluation—students' open-ended comments. These remarks attribute improvement in overall language skills as well as success in the content course to the language course; additionally students report improved self-esteem.

Potential Breakdowns in the Adjunct Model

As we have reported, participant response to FSP has been overwhelmingly positive, yet we feel that it is equally important in our analysis to pinpoint areas in the adjunct model where breakdowns can occur. More than anything else, the success of the adjunct model rests on the strength of the various coordination meetings held before and during the term. Coordination problems have arisen due to staff turnover and inefficient meetings. A second potential problem area can develop when the underlying philosophy of the program is either not shared by all instructors or not communicated uniformly to the students. For example, one year we seemed to be at cross purposes with the content course professor who, in his eagerness to create a nonthreatening learning environment, tended to minimize the students' academic responsibilities. We felt undermined by the professor's casual approach and, more importantly, felt that his attitude provided a misleading impression of future academic demands. Assignment planning is the third area of potential conflict. Because preparing students for examinations and papers requires the collective effort of both staffs, all assignments must be carefully planned by content and language instructors.

The final area of potential breakdown is a consequence of the structure of the adjunct model at UCLA. As mentioned, both native English speakers and ESL students participate in FSP, but there are many more sections of English composition than of ESL. Within the language adjunct, then, the ESL instructors are always in the minority. At times we have felt that neither the English nor content course staffs really understand the particular dynamics of working with an ESL population. We have been overruled on several important decisions regarding textbook selection, assignment construction, and grading criteria. These kinds of clashes, while annoying, are probably inevitable when different interests are represented in a single program. Moreover, we feel that the advantages of this set-up, which allow native speaker/nonnative speaker interaction, far outnumber any of the disadvantages.

Applications of the Adjunct Model

It is evident from the preceding discussion that several factors may limit the applicability of the adjunct model. Because the model depends on the availability of content course offerings, a full-blown adjunct model is probably not feasible at an intensive language institute. Further, as we have described it, adjunct instruction assumes that students can cope (with assistance from the language and content staff) with authentic readings and lectures in the content course. Thus, the model is not applicable to beginning proficiency levels. Finally, the model requires an administration willing to fund the large network of instructors and staff needed as well as the language teacher's commitment of time and energy to integrate content materials with language teaching aims. This effective coordinating effort behind the model may not be possible in all settings.

Despite these limitations, we believe the adjunct model can be adapted to fit other institutional settings and populations. As evidence of this, adjunct programs such as FSP at UCLA or modified adjuncts—i.e., language workshops attached to a content course—currently exist both here and abroad: with undergraduate international students studying Human Geography (Peterson, 1985) at Macalester College in St. Paul, Minnesota and graduate students in Pharmacy (Seal, 1985) and Business Law (Snow and Brinton, 1984) at the University of Southern California; with foreign students studying the Philosophy of Science (Jonas & Li, 1983), American History and Economics (Spencer, 1986) in the People's Republic of China; and finally with both francophone and anglophone students at the bilingual University of Ottawa (Wesche, 1985) learning the second language through subject matter courses such as Psychology and History.

Conclusions

The adjunct model of language instruction provides an ideal framework for an English for Academic Purposes setting. With the focus in the language class on essential modes of academic writing, academic reading and study skill development, and treatment of persistent structural errors, students are being prepared to transfer these skills to the content course. The activities of the content-based language class are geared to stimulate students to think and learn in the target language by requiring them to synthesize information from the content-area lectures and readings. Because these materials provide authentic content for students to discuss and write about, the model provides a context for integrating the four traditional language skills. An underlying assumption in this pedagogical framework is that student motivation in the language class will increase in direct proportion to the relevance of its activities, and, in turn, student success in the content course will reflect the carefully coordinated efforts of this team approach. Our experience as instructors confirms this assumption. Furthermore, the adjunct model offers ESL students a critical, but often neglected option. It gives them access to native-speaker interaction and the authentic, unsimplified language of academic texts and lectures in the content course while enabling them to benefit from sheltered ESL instruction which meets their particular language needs.

References

Anderson, J., Eisenburg, N., Holland, J. Wiener, H., & Rivera-Kron, C. (1983). *Integrated skills reinforcement: Reading, writing, speaking, and listening across the curriculum*. New York: Longman.

Bullock Report. (1975). *A language for life*. London: HMSO.

Jonas, D., & Li, X. L. (1983). *The revised adjunct concept in China*. Paper presented at TESOL '83, Toronto, Canada.

Peterson, P. W. (1985). The bridge course: Listening comprehension in authentic settings. *TESOL Newsletter, 19*, 21.

Rhodes, N. C., & Schreibstein, A. R. (1983). *Foreign language in the elementary school: A practical guide*. Washington, DC: Center for Applied Linguistics.

Rose, M. (1980). Teaching university discourse. *Teaching/Writing/Learning*. Canadian Council of Teachers of English monograph.

Rose, M. (1982). *UCLA's Freshman Summer Program: A description of the English composition component*. Unpublished manuscript, University of California, Los Angeles.

Seal, B. D. (1985). *Some observations on adjunct courses*. Paper presented at CATESOL '85, San Diego, California.

Snow, M. A., & Brinton, D. (1984). *Linking ESL courses with university content courses: The adjunct model*. ERIC Document Reproduction Service No. ED 244 515.

Spencer, L. (1986). *An adjunct model ESP program: Balancing content and skills*. Paper presented at TESOL '86, Anaheim, California.

Sutton, M. (1978). The writing adjunct program at the Small College of California State College, Dominguez Hills. In Jasper P. Neal (Ed.), *Options for the teaching of English: Freshman composition*, Modern Language Association.

Wesche, M. B. (1985). Immersion and the universities. *Canadian Modern Language Review, 41*, 931-940.

Widdowson, H. (1978). *Teaching language as communication*. Oxford: Oxford University.

Widdowson, H. (1983). *Learning purpose and language use*. New York: Oxford University.

Appendix

FSP Course Evaluation Instrument

PART A

1. I feel I was placed _____ in this course.
   Too High   About Right   Too Low   No Answer

2. In terms of difficulty this course was _____ .

Too Hard	About Right	Too Easy	No Answer
1.42	93.47	4.26	0.85 percent

3. I spent _____ hours/week preparing for this English course.
   2-4   4-6   6-9   9-12   12-16   more   No Answer

4. The instructor was enthusiastic about teaching the course.
   Strongly agree   Agree   No opinion   Disagree   Strongly disagree   No ans

5. The instructor seemed genuinely interested in the students' progress.
   Strongly agree   Agree   No opinion   Disagree   Strongly disagree   No ans

6. The instructor thoroughly understood the materials in this course.
   Strongly agree   Agree   No opinion   Disagree   Strongly disagree   No ans

7. Class presentations were carefully organized and clearly delivered.
   Strongly agree   Agree   No opinion   Disagree   Strongly disagree   No ans

8. The instructor made students feel welcome in seeking help.
   Strongly agree   Agree   No opinion   Disagree   Strongly disagree   No ans

9. I would like to take another course from this instructor.
   Strongly agree   Agree   No opinion   Disagree   Strongly disagree   No ans

10. I am a better writer than when I entered FSP.
    Strongly agree   Agree   No opinion   Disagree   Strongly disagree   No ans

11. This course helped me write better papers for my breadth course.
    Strongly agree   Agree   No opinion   Disagree   Strongly disagree   No ans

12. This course helped me read my breadth course texts more effectively.
    Strongly agree   Agree   No opinion   Disagree   Strongly disagree   No ans

13. The English textbook I used helped improve my writing.
    Strongly agree   Agree   No opinion   Disagree   Strongly disagree   No ans

14. My overall rating of this course.
    Very High   High   Medium   Low   Very Low   No ans

15. My overall rating of the instructor.
    Very High   High   Medium   Low   Very Low   No ans

PART B

How students rated the effectiveness of:

written comments on papers
Didn't rely   Vry Helpful   Helpful   So-so   Nt vry hlpfl   No Good   No ans

class discussion
Didn't rely   Vry Helpful   Helpful   So-so   Nt vry hlpfl   No Good   No ans

presentations of other students
Didn't rely   Vry Helpful   Helpful   So-so   Nt vry hlpfl   No Good   No ans

lectures on grammar, style, etc.
Didn't rely   Vry Helpful   Helpful   So-so   Nt vry hlpfl   No Good   No ans

small peer editing groups
Didn't rely   Vry Helpful   Helpful   So-so   Nt vry hlpfl   No Good   No ans

grammar exercises
Didn't rely   Vry Helpful   Helpful   So-so   Nt vry hlpfl   No Good   No ans

in-class writing
Didn't rely   Vry Helpful   Helpful   So-so   Nt vry hlpfl   No Good   No ans

take home writing assignments
Didn't rely   Vry Helpful   Helpful   So-so   Nt vry hlpfl   No Good   No ans

discussions of study skills and reading skills
Didn't rely   Vry Helpful   Helpful   So-so   Nt vry hlpfl   No Good   No ans

individual conferences with the teacher
Didn't rely   Vry Helpful   Helpful   So-so   Nt vry hlpfl   No Good   No ans

writing assignments NOT connected to the breadth course materials
Didn't rely   Vry Helpful   Helpful   So-so   Nt vry hlpfl   No Good   No ans

writing assignments connected to the breadth course materials
Didn't rely   Vry Helpful   Helpful   So-so   Nt vry hlpfl   No Good   No ans

work on prewriting and planning
Didn't rely   Vry Helpful   Helpful   So-so   Nt vry hlpfl   No Good   No ans

work on revising
Didn't rely   Vry Helpful   Helpful   So-so   Nt vry hlpfl   No Good   No ans

freewriting
Didn't rely   Vry Helpful   Helpful   So-so   Nt vry hlpfl   No Good   No ans

other
Didn't rely   Vry Helpful   Helpful   So-so   Nt vry hlpfl   No Good   No ans

About the Authors

Marguerite Ann Snow (PhD, Applied Linguistics, University of California, Los Angeles, 1985) pursued her research interests in immersion foreign language education, English grammar, and language teaching methodology at UCLA. Dr. Snow has worked with both native English-speaking and ESL university students, developing content-based English curricula, and has taught adult ESL in Los Angeles since 1979. She has presented papers at many conferences, including AILA, TESOL, and ACTFL, and she has published her research in *Second Language Acquisition Studies* (Newbury House, 1983), several professional journals, and in reports to the U.S. Department of Education (Grant No. 660-182-01527) and to the National Institute of Education. In the fall of 1985 she was a Fulbright Scholar at the Chinese University of Hong Kong in the Department of Linguistics and Language Teaching. Currently, she is a Visiting Assistant Professor in the Linguistics Department at UCLA.

Donna M. Brinton (MA, TESL, University of California, Los Angeles, 1980) serves as Lecturer and Audio-Visual Coordinator for the TESL/Applied Linguistics at UCLA. She began her ESL career by teaching general EFL and ESP courses in Germany and has continued to be involved in ESL instruction and teacher training since coming to the Los Angeles area in 1976. Her primary interests are curriculum design, materials development, accent improvement, and instructional technology. For the past five years she has taught in a content-based summer program for incoming freshmen at UCLA. Ms. Brinton has presented papers at TESOL, CCCC, and a number of California educational association conferences and has published her research in *TESOL Quarterly*. She is a contributor to *Foreign Teaching Assistants in U.S. Universities* (NAFSA, 1984) and the coauthor of *Getting along: English grammar and writing* (Prentice-Hall, 1982).

Linking Content and Language Teachers: Collaboration Across the Curriculum

Sarah Benesch

College of Staten Island, City University of New York

Abstract

The paper describes a study of the interdisciplinary collaboration among three faculty members, one from psychology and two from English, who taught a block of three linked courses, Freshman Social Science, ESL Reading, and ESL Writing, at an urban college. The data included notes of weekly meetings and interviews, assignments, and students papers. The paper documents solutions created collaboratively by the three instructors to deal with pedagogical problems that arose during the semester in which their courses were blocked. Because the three worked well together, their experience can serve as an example of successful collaboration between ESL and content faculty.

Linking Content and Language Teachers: Collaboration Across the Curriculum

The writing-across-the-curriculum movement has encouraged dialogue and, in many cases, collaboration between faculty in different departments. A guiding assumption of this movement is that because language is central to all fields of study, reading and writing must receive the attention of faculty in every department (Britton, Burgess, Martin, McLeod, & Rosen, 1975; Fulwiler & Young, 1982). ESL faculty in American colleges, acknowledging the obligation to alert colleagues in other departments to the special problems of nonnative students and recognizing the need to become more aware of what goes on in these students' content courses, have joined the cross-curricular dialogue. The goals of this dialogue range from information-gathering about the curriculum and pedagogy of the existing language and content courses (Johns, 1981) to devising ways to create and sustain cross-curricular links (Dick & Esch, 1985).

The Freshman Workshop Program

The focus of this paper is the interdisciplinary collaboration that took place over the course of a semester at the College of Staten Island (CSI), City University of New York (CUNY) among three faculty members, two from the English department, and one from psychology, who taught a block of three linked courses: ESL Reading, ESL Writing, and Freshman Social Science. These three courses formed one of four blocks offered during the fall, 1985 semester in the CSI Freshman Workshop Program (FWP), designed for native and nonnative students who fail the CUNY Reading, Writing, and Math Assessment Tests. Like the UCLA Freshman Summer Program, the FWP evolved from a recognition that many freshmen are unused to taking an active role in their own learning and that many come to college with little experience in certain linguistic and academic activities such as reading critically, taking notes from readings and lectures, formulating questions, and writing coherent essays. The philosophy of the FWP is that when students are encouraged to speak, read, and write extensively about their academic subjects, they are more involved with and gain greater understanding of the content (Mayher, Lester, &

Pradl, 1983; Marland, 1977; Wotring & Tierney, 1981). Students in the FWP may choose from four content areas—social science, science and technology, humanities, or business— each of which is paired with a reading and a writing course.

The pairing of content and language courses, described here and in other papers in this volume, acknowledges that English and content-area departments play complementary roles in providing instruction. The linguistic activities used by English faculty are tools for learning content, and the theories and concepts of partic- ular disciplines are the subjects for student discussion, writing, and reading.

The FWP is based on another assumption: Not only students but also their professors need greater awareness of the demands of college study. The program therefore includes a semester-long weekly seminar, the Developmental Education Study Group (DESG), in which faculty who will be teaching in the program become students, reading and writing about unfamiliar material from various content areas and discussing their observations about the relationship between language and learning. In addition, while teaching in the program, FWP faculty are given one credit hour of released time to meet weekly with the other members of their block to plan writing and reading assignments, to discuss students' progress, and to shape a coordinated syllabus. The choice of course material is left to block members.

Studying Faculty Collaboration

The data which form the basis of this paper include notes taken at the weekly meetings of the block studied, notes taken during interviews with block members, assignments, and student papers. The purpose of examining this collaboration was to discover how faculty in different departments develop joint syllabi and assign- ments, while their linked courses are in progress, to enhance their students' content and language learning. This paper documents solutions created collaboratively by three instructors to deal with pedagogical problems that arose during the semester. Because the three worked well together, their experience can serve as an example of successful collaboration across disciplines.

The greatest challenge of the collaboration among the members of the block was to reconcile the instructional goals and methods of a typical introductory psychology class with those of ESL reading and writing classes. Faculty who teach freshman-level content courses normally use lectures and textbooks to convey information about key concepts in the introductory curriculum. They test students' understanding of concepts by eliciting answers to teacher-generated questions and by administering midterm and final examinations. The goals of language courses, on the other hand, are not to teach and test specific information but rather to have students talk, read, and write extensively to gain greater fluency, clarity, and accuracy in using language. Given these differences in goals and methods, it is not surprising that during the first weeks of the semester, the social science professor focused on content and the English professors on linguistic processes. As the semester progressed, however, the three instructors developed language-based assignments which were used in each of the classes to promote greater understanding of the social science concepts.

Establishing a Climate for Learning

Because there was no predetermined syllabus or textbook to dictate the course material and its sequence or speed of presentation, the social science professor experimented at the beginning of the semester with the following method of selecting topics:

> On the first day of class, I asked the students if they had any questions they thought a social scientist could answer. It took two weeks for them to understand that question, but they began to come up with issues that affect their own lives . . . . They gave me a range of issues, and I clustered these into a few topics. (I. Smodlaka, personal communication, Dec, 1985)

Allowing students to choose what they would study represented a change for this professor, whose introductory course syllabus usually consisted of preselected topics to be studied during predetermined time periods, regardless of the students' pace of learning. By clustering the students' choices into a few topics, he created a syllabus that was less crowded, more flexible, and responsive to students' interests and concerns.

Just as the social science professor spent the first weeks of the semester determining, with the students, the content of the workshop, so the two English professors fostered what Torbe and Medway (1981) call a "climate for learning." The ESL reading instructor highlighted aspects of the reading process, designed, in her words, "to wean them away from their dictionaries" and "get them to engage with text," such as anticipating what will happen next, bringing interest to reading rather than demanding that the text be intrinsically interesting, becoming aware of the images

evoked by the text, and identifying areas in the text where comprehension breaks down] During the first few weeks in the writing
class, students were encouraged to write about and share former
experiences with writing, do freewriting and active listening, respond
to one of the teacher's drafts, form peer response groups, and
revise first drafts.

Talking to Learn

To present various topics, the social science professor used films
and lectures followed by class discussion of basic concepts. He had
been attracted to the technique, introduced in the DESG, of
increasing student understanding of new material by having them
cast it into their own language. As a psychologist, he subscribed to
the notion that individuals understand best that which they are
allowed to articulate and sort out in their own words. Class discussions, however, proved to be more difficult than he had anticipated. His open-ended questioning had not stimulated critical
responses to the first film, a problem he brought up during a block
meeting. The English professors, acting as language consultants,
suggested that because the film presented new material, the students would need multiple opportunities to talk about these concepts, not only in whole class but also in small group discussions.
(For more on the relationship between talking and learning, see
the Hirsch article.)

The pedagogical issue here was how to encourage the type of
talk that would allow students to make unfamiliar material their
own. The content area instructor had to learn to give students
more time to discuss new material among themselves. He also had
to accept that their responses to the films would not necessarily be
those he had anticipated. This issue arose during another block
meeting when the social science professor reported that after
listening to the students discuss a film on perception, "Eye of the
Beholder," he felt they "[didn't] pay attention to essential points."
Again, their responses were not those he had anticipated, and he
was therefore concerned that students had neither understood the
film nor grasped the concepts illustrated. These comments prompted
semester-long dialogue about how the viewer, or reader, makes
meaning and how the teacher facilitates meaning-making. The
dialogue centered on two questions: (1) Where does meaning
reside? and (2) How can teachers accept students' initial responses
and then promote deeper understanding and more articulate and
critical responses?

At subsequent block meetings, the English professors brought

up the concept of reader/writer/text interactions to discuss the
issues of making and deriving meaning through reading and writing. This concept is well- summarized by Tierney and Spiro (1979)
in one of the many articles assigned as part of the DESG curriculum:

> Reading comprehension can . . . be characterized as invol-
> ving and being influenced by the interaction back and
> forth among (a) the text; (b) the reader, including the
> reader's background of experience and assumptions about
> the author's intentions, interests, etc.; and (c) the strate-
> gies the reader employs (consciously or not) to mediate
> between the other two components. . . . The text is like a
> blueprint that guides the construction of understanding.
> (p. 133)

The concept of "the text acting as a blueprint that guides the
construction of meaning" resonated strongly for the content teacher
who immediately found parallel concepts in psychology: projec-
tion, impression formation, and denotative vs. connotative meaning.

Collaborative Assignments

The reading and writing instructors not only initiated discussion
about reader/writer/text interaction and meaning-making during
the weekly block meetings but also developed practical language-
based assignments to increase student participation in their learning of social science content. Of all the assignments made, two
stand out for their success in enhancing deeper understanding of
material presented through films and discussion. The first was
about obedience, and the second, prejudice.

During the third week of the semester, the students saw a film
in their social science class about Stanley Milgrim's famous experiment on obedience which tested ". . . how much pain an ordinary
citizen would inflict on another person simply because he was
ordered to by an experimental scientist." The experiment demonstrated that ". . . authority won more often than not" (p. 793). At
the block meeting, the teachers discussed the division between
students who were horrified that the subjects of the experiment
had been capable of subordinating their empathy to obedience and
students who thought, perhaps because the experiment was presented in filmed version, that it was fictitious. An important impli-
cation of the experiment, that when obedience and morality come
into conflict, most of us would probably obey, was lost on the
group. Students did not relate Milgrim's findings to their own

lives; the experiment was academic information that did not inspire critical thinking.

The three teachers, agreeing that the students needed to study the experiment more carefully, and from a personal angle, created two additional assignments, one for the reading class and one for the writing class. The reading assignment was an essay by Milgrim explaining the design, procedures, and results of the experiment in greater detail, and, more importantly, in anecdotal fashion. After students read, discussed, and compared the article to the filmed account, they were given a writing assignment aimed at a more personal exploration of obedience. They were asked to describe an experience in which they had had to choose whether or not to obey someone in a position of authority, such as a teacher or family member, and to explain what they had done and why. This assignment had universal application. None of the students had trouble remembering such an episode. Although most of the students had been incredulous when reading about the degree of obedience of Milgrim's subjects, the majority of them described an incident in which they had obeyed an authority figure because the social structure in the environment seemed to give them no choice. By examining experiences which led them to decide whether or not to obey, students were forced to confront the factors leading to such decisions and the tendency of most humans to choose the path of least resistance, obedience.

A Nigerian student wrote about obeying his older brother's continuous requests to run errands for him even though my student had to miss school, which he loved. Apparently, skipping school produced less dangerous consequences than would have disobeying the older brother. While my student rebelled inwardly, his compliance belied his resentment and frustration. The most successful responses to this assignment not only described an experience but also analyzed the reasons for the student's behavior. For example, a Korean student recounted how he had obeyed his mother and reflected that he had complied not because he agreed with her but because he was then only 12 years old and still financially dependent on his family. Here is an excerpt from the first draft:

> First, I didn't want to eat that medicine. And second I didn't feel good after I ate the medicine. But my mom strongly believed the medicine's effect against the allergy even I told to her it didn't work to me. I didn't want to eat anymore this medicine but my mom strongly ordered to me. Finally, I ate that medicine almost 4 months until

the allergy gone from me. So I obeyed my mom's order. I couldn't refuse that because my mom told me if I don't eat that medicine, I couldn't get anything from mom. I mean she don't want to pay for my baseball equipment, books, and recorder player etc. After 9 months the allergy was gone from me. I thought the time made it. But my mom believed the medicine made it. What could I do? I was too young to disobey and I needed so many things wich I had to get money from my mom for buy it.

The benefit of this writing assignment was that some of the students who could not understand or believe the magnitude of obedience to authority in Milgrim's subjects, acknowledged their own tendency to obey. Without the vehicle of linked content and language courses, the students would have had no opportunity to explore the topic in depth. Instead, they would have followed their teacher on to the next topic on the syllabus.

The writing assignment on prejudice stemmed from the teachers' concern that although students had asked to study prejudice because of the negative reception they often received as foreigners, some had demonstrated intolerance for the ideas and cultures of fellow students. The teachers wanted students to explore both their prejudicial feelings towards others and those that others exhibited towards them. The content teacher worked on the first by having students write descriptions of an American, share their descriptions, and discuss the stereotypes appearing in their writing, thereby forcing an awareness of their own prejudices. The writing teacher opted to have students explore prejudicial feelings directed toward them through an assignment, proposed by Ponsot and Deen (1982), which calls for the writer to "correct a misconception or nail a stereotype with firsthand knowledge." The writer generates ideas for the essay by completing the following sentence: "They say _____, but my experience tells me _____." One student began, "They say that all Puerto Ricans are lazy, but my father and I work very hard." He gave evidence of their diligence by describing his and his father's various jobs. A few of the Haitians wrote about their problem dealing with people who believe they have AIDS. A Japanese woman wrote that American men view her as someone whose only ambition is to serve her husband unquestioningly. The greatest benefit of this assignment came when papers were shared because prejudices held by individuals toward the various cultures and religions represented in the class surfaced and were discussed. Although students did not shed their prejudices, they were at least led to recognize and consider them.

Conclusion

The preceding examples illustrate the greatest advantage of combining content and language teaching: When courses are linked, the *teachers* are linked and they can consult one another about how to increase the students' ability to make new knowledge familiar. Content area teachers know the important concepts and literature of their discipline. Language teachers know how to use reading, writing, and speaking to facilitate the learning of unfamiliar material. Linking this complementary expertise is a powerful pedagogical formula to strengthen the curriculum by providing opportunities for faculty to see connections between their respective fields, report to one another on students' progress, and work together to devise solutions to curricular problems.

The collaboration in the ESL Reading/ESL Writing/Social Science block described in this article deepened the professors' understanding of the relationship between modern composition theory, reader response theory, and psychological concepts; sharpened their awareness of students' backgrounds and learning styles; and enhanced their facility to create and revise assignments that combine content and language teaching.

Recommendations

Those contemplating setting up and running a linkage program should anticipate certain administrative hurdles, such as how to provide released time for faculty development seminars and weekly meetings and how to convince deans, department heads, and faculty that linkage is worthwhile. The training of faculty across disciplines presents other challenges. How, for example, can the various teaching and classroom management techniques used by different faculty members—lectures, peer group collaboration, multiple choice exams, journals, grammar exercises, research papers, textbook selections, primary source material—be reconciled? And how can faculty be encouraged to put aside preconceptions and old syllabi to be guided by students' questions and interests?

While linking content and language courses could exacerbate interdepartmental tensions and conflicts about teaching theories, methods, and materials, it can also promote rich dialogue across the curriculum. If faculty participation is voluntary, if participants are given time to study the relationship between language and learning, if administrative problems are resolved, and if faculty are encouraged to collaborate regularly, linked courses can facilitate student learning.

References

Britton, J., Burgess, T., Martin, N., McLeod, A., & Rosen, H. (1975). *The development of writing abilities* (pp. 11-18). London: Macmillan Education.

Dick, J. A. R., & Esch, R. M. (1985). Dialogues among the disciplines: A plan for faculty discussions of writing across the curriculum. *College Composition and Communication, 36*, 178-182.

Fulwiler, T., & Young, A. (1982). *Language connections: Reading and writing across the curriculum.* Urbana, IL: National Council of Teachers of English.

Johns, A. M. (1981). Necessary English: A faculty survey. *TESOL Quarterly, 15*, 51-57.

Marland, M. (1977). *Language across the curriculum.* London: Heinemann Educational Books.

Mayher, J. S., Lester, N., & Pradl, G. M. (1983). *Learning to write/writing to learn.* Montclair, NJ: Boynton/Cook.

Milgrim, S. (1980). The perils of obedience. In A. M. Eastman (Gen. Ed.), *The Norton Reader.* New York: W. W. Norton & Co.

Ponsot, M., & Deen, R. (1982). *Beat not the poor desk.* Montclair, NJ: Boynton/Cook.

Tierney, R. J., & Spiro, R. J. (1979). Some basic notions about reading comprehension: Implications for teachers. In J. Harste & R. Cary (Eds.) *New Perspectives on Comprehension* (pp. 133-138). Bloomington, IN: Indiana University Press.

Torbe, M., & Medway, P. (1981). *The climate for learning.* Montclair, NJ: Boynton/Cook.

Wotring, A. M., & Tierney, R. (1981). *Two studies of writing in high school science.* Berkeley: Bay Area Writing Project.

About the Author

Sarah Benesch is Assistant Professor of English at the College of Staten Island, City University of New York. She is coauthor of two composition textbooks for ESL students, *Academic Writing Workshop,* (with Mia Rakijas and Betsy Rorschach) and *Academic Writing Workshop II* (with Betsy Rorschach), published by Wadsworth, 1986 and 1988. Professor Benesch has presented papers at TESOL and CCCC on collaborative learning, linking content and language, and using microcomputers to teach writing to ESL college students. She is currently President of the City University of New York ESL Council (1987-1988).

Author's Note

The author would like to acknowledge Professor Rose Katz Ortiz, the creator and director of the Freshman Workshop Program and the Development Education Study Group, and Maryann Castelucci and Peter Miller, the codirectors of the CSI Collaborative Learning Group. She would also like to thank Professors Ortiz, Cornwell, and Smodlaka for their collegiality and feedback.

Language Across the Curriculum:
A Model for ESL Students in Content Courses

Linda Hirsch

Hostos Community College, City University of New York

Abstract

Nonnative college students are often not ready to compete successfully with their native counterparts in subject area courses even after completing a sequence of ESL courses. A tutoring model was developed, funded, and tested to correct this problem. This model assigns ESL students to small tutor-led groups centered on particular content courses. Guided by a trained tutor, students meet once a week and use talking and writing as learning tools to increase their comprehension of course material while improving their oral and written English-language skills. The success of this model is discussed.

Language Across the Curriculum:
A Model for ESL Students in Content Courses

Project Overview

In fall 1982, Hostos Community College, an urban bilingual college of the City University of New York, received a 2-year grant from the Fund for the Improvement of Postsecondary Education (FIPSE) to study the English language difficulties of adult, advanced, or post-ESL students in content area courses. The project developed a cost-effective tutoring model which recognized that although these students had completed an ESL sequence of study, they were often unable to compete successfully with native speakers of English in subject area courses. They could not understand the English used in lectures and textbooks and thus could not grasp the course content. Their subsequent poor grades in these courses frequently led to a pronounced sense of failure and a tendency to abandon their studies. It was the project's overarching goal to help these students succeed and ultimately attain their career goals. While this problem is particularly significant to Hostos with an incoming freshman class that is 63% Spanish-dominant, it is also a problem of growing national importance because increasing numbers of nonnative speakers of English are entering our school systems.

To address the ESL student's cognitive difficulties in content courses, the tutoring model assigned students to small tutor-led groups centered on a particular course such as General Biology, Introduction to Business, or Early Childhood Education. Guided by a trained tutor, students met once a week for 1½ hours during the 14-week academic semester. They used talking and writing as tools to increase their comprehension of course material while seeking to improve their oral and written English-language skills. Because of this model's proven success (see *Evaluation*), it has been widely implemented throughout the college and today serves approximately 250 students per year.

Theoretical Background

The tutoring model rests on the assumption that language may be used for different purposes, one of which is learning. Much of the literature proposes that writing has a heuristic function; it is a

71

way of knowing and a unique tool for learning. The model is partly rooted in the current writing-across-the-curriculum movement which recognizes that writing is a means of learning subject matter. Yet much of the research examines not just the value of writing throughout the curriculum, but of talking as well, emphasizing the interaction between the two and their significance for learning. Drawing on this research, the model incorporates not only principles of writing across the curriculum, but also of language across the curriculum as vehicles for ESL students to learn content and, in particular, that kind of language termed *expressive*.

Expressive language is defined by James Britton (1975) as language closest to natural speech. Britton explains that expressive speech is "utterance at its most relaxed and intimate, as free as possible from outside demands, whether those of a task or of an audience" (p. 82). It is language close to the speaker, and unlike the more public "transactional function," whose purpose is to convey information, expressive language focuses on fluency rather than on explicitness or correctness. Britton maintains that it is in expressive speech that we are likely to rehearse the growing points of our formulation and analysis of experience. Expressive language reveals the thinking process. It is a means by which the new is tentatively explored and is related to what is already known. It is the function through which we frame ideas and express tentative conclusions. Because expressive language is a powerful tool that externalizes our first stages in solving a problem, it is the means by which participating ESL students manipulate and learn the subject matter of their content area course.

The model also reflects research which suggests that learning is an active, ongoing process in which an individual mind makes meaning from experience (Berthoff, 1981; Britton, 1970; Kelly, 1963) and that language—both talking and writing—plays an important role. In this view, learning is more than the passive acceptance of factual material. Knowledge, it holds, can not be given; pupils must make it for themselves. Learning is dependent upon students' abilities to make connections between new material and their existing understanding. Through talking and writing, especially expressive talking and writing, students are able to formulate conceptions and make connections between new knowledge and what they already know (Britton, Burgess, Martin, McLeod, & Rosen, 1975; Martin, D'Arcy, Newton, & Parker, 1976). True learning can occur only when students are able to engage material in a personally meaningful way on the basis of previous experience and make it their own through the use of their immediate language resources (Britton, 1982; Torbe & Medway, 1981). This view of learning also holds that teachers and students are partners in the learning process and that teachers provide a context for a more genuine kind of learning. They are fellow inquirers rather than evaluators. They create an environment that encourages the active use of pupils' language in the classroom (Barnes, Britton, & Rosen, 1969; Burgess et al., 1973; Martin et al., 1976).

The tutoring model incorporates the use of language for learning in a student-centered learning environment and applies these principles to adult ESL students across the curriculum. During group sessions participants are given sufficient opportunities for expressive, exploratory talk and writing. Tutors play a less dominant role in the learning process by encouraging students to learn from each other through reciprocal discussion and shared writings. Individual sessions might find students paraphrasing concepts, using learning logs, writing tutor- or pupil-generated assignments, reading from their papers, or holding frequent group discussions. Thus a group that spends one session drafting and revising written work might devote itself to discussion during the next. The format and subject of each session are determined by the needs of the students and the demands of the particular course.

Student Selection

Students are selected from among registrants in those English-language content courses that contain large numbers of ESL students concurrently registered in Advanced ESL (ESL 1332) or Basic Composition (ENG 1300). The latter is a transitional composition course specifically designed for second language students who have completed the college's ESL sequence but do not yet have the writing skills required for admission into Freshman Composition (ENG 1302). These content courses encompass a wide range of liberal arts offerings and have included Introduction to Business, General Biology, Introduction to Political Economy, Introduction to Social Science, American Government, Micro-Economics, and Child Developmental Psychology. Tutoring has also been provided to advanced and intermediate ESL students who are seeking entry to the professional health care field and are enrolled in specifically designed content courses. Students are assigned to groups on the basis of a common free period during which at least three and no more than eight are able to meet.

Tutor Selection and Training

Because tutors are an essential component of this model, their selection and training are crucial to its success. Tutors are selected from within and outside the college, based on their knowledge of the content discipline and their proven abilities as writers. While the project subsequently trains tutors to provide a more student-centered, language-rich learning environment, tutors have to enter the project with those personal qualities that enhance tutor effectiveness such as friendliness, warmth, and a desire to work with others.

Given that the average Hostos student is 27 years old, the tutors chosen have been graduate as well as undergraduate students. They have come to the project with diverse academic backgrounds. For example, Allison was a junior at Barnard majoring in English and planning a career in law. Yamila, a communications major, had a BA from New York University. Jennice was receiving her MA in political science from New York University, and Lynn was completing her MA in communications at Fordham University. Thomas had received his BA in English and philosophy from Bard College, and Stephen had his BA in philosophy from Stroudsburg State College. Joseph was a history major at Hunter College and Dominique an education graduate student at Bank Street. Ivania, a former Hostos student, was completing her undergraduate work at The City College, and Christine, a senior at Fordham University, was majoring in business and finance.

Tutors participate in intensive, ongoing training to prepare for their roles as facilitators of student learning. As an integral part of this training, tutors meet as a group under the leadership of the project director, 12 hours a week, for 3 weeks prior to group assignment and thereafter once a week for 1½ hours. They work together to formulate ideas on topics generated by the group leader, group interaction, or content faculty with project participants. Tutors discuss ideas, write drafts of papers using expressive mode discourse, and occasionally present final versions of papers in the transactional function. Thus the group provides tutors with the first-hand experience they will need to lead their own groups. Specifically, tutors are helped to gain awareness of themselves as writers and of their composing processes, to understand the importance of oral discourse as a means of exploring and formulating new ideas, to familiarize themselves with the uses of Britton's expressive mode speech and writing, and to appreciate the tutor's role as facilitator of the group learning process.

Basic texts for tutor training are *The Tutor Book* (Arkin & Shollar) and *Learning to Write/Writing to Learn* (Mayher, Lester, & Pradl). In addition, tutors read and discuss research on second-language acquisition, the composing process, and writing across the curriculum. (Appendix A lists research read by tutors.) They are required to keep a journal (a traditional vehicle for expressive mode discourse) on their tutoring experiences, and weekly training sessions enable them to share problems and successes as well as to obtain support and feedback on their work as leaders of peer learning groups. Tutors are observed and evaluated by the project director and are closely monitored to see that they are comfortable with their tasks and are providing students the opportunity to help themselves and each other.

To ensure that tutors are exposed to various methodologies, independent consultants have led training sessions on such topics as:

a) Using a conferencing model in small groups and individualizing writing instructions;
b) Role-playing and response techniques;
c) The development of writing abilities and the writing process;
d) The functions of writing (expressive, transactional, and poetic);
e) A guide to writing assignments across the curriculum;
f) Strategies for modeling responses and getting writers to be readers of their own texts;
g) Helping writers move from expressive writing to transactional writing;
h) Problem solving through talking and writing;
i) The value of writing in responding to reading;
j) Using writing to motivate and synthesize learning;
k) Listening comprehension in ESL;
l) Improving reading comprehension in content courses.

In addition to facilitating peer learning groups and participating in training sessions, tutors perform other tasks. Primary of these is the development of curriculum materials to improve student understanding of course material. Working with the Project Director, tutors have designed a variety of curriculum aids including study guides, "writing to learn" assignments, and vocabulary reviews. These materials are a direct response to student needs and incorporate principles of language for learning. In addition, once a week tutors attend the students' content area class. This ensures that tutors are aware of the material covered and of the instructors' expectations of student performance. This attendance also provides for greater continuity between content class and tutoring group activities. Tutors also maintain office hours (1½ hours per group) for individual conferences. Tutors are required to submit detailed accounts of each group session reporting discussions, written work including mode and peer response, significant aspects of each individual's participation, and an overall assessment of the session. Tutors are also expected to meet with content faculty who have project participants to inform instructors about student performance and to obtain faculty input about topics for group discussion. Most tutors work 15 hours a week and run no more than two groups.

From Theory to Practice

The preceding project description outlined the model's theoretical framework and implementation, but it can not fully convey how this learning model actually operates. The following transcript and analysis are provided to reveal what occurs in a student-centered tutoring session in which language plays a dominant role. The students' and tutor's own words reveal the ways in which expressive talk and writing enhance student learning.

Excerpt from General Biology Learning Group

April 15, 1983 — Allison, tutor

A: What are you confused about?

M: Tissues.

A: Can you explain to Virginia what you know about tissues? Start with epithelial tissue.

5   M: Epithelial tissue made up of flat sheets.

A: Why don't you draw a diagram on the board.

(Maria did not seem keen on this suggestion and approached the board hesitantly.)

A: How about writing down the three questions you
10 should ask about the various kinds of tissues?

(N.B. Based on last week's session)

Maria wrote:

How is look like?

What is the function?

15 Where is founded?

(Allison corrected the "how" to "what" but left the other questions as written.)

Maria turned to the board.

20 M: The function of the epithelial tissue is to give support, protection.

A: To what?

Maria read a passage from the textbook.

A: Could you put that in your own words?

Maria went to the board and drew a diagram.

25 M: What you name the hair?

A: Cilia. Good. Where is it found?

M: Mucous.

A: What is the organ where cilia is? Where is it?

M: Throat.

30 A: Cilia are also in the lungs. Tell Virginia [n.b.: who was absent the session before] about epithelial tissue in the lungs.

M: When all the dirt comes in, the cilia move it out.

A: (To Virginia) Do you understand that? What did she
35 say?

V: The cilia move out the dirt.

A: (To Virginia) What organ are cilia found in?

V: Lungs.

A: Good. It's also in other places. It's in a variety of
40 organs. Do you know?

(There are six seconds of silence)

M: The stomach, intestines.

A: Good! Very good!

Maria then read a sentence from the text which said that
45 epithelial tissue was found in the boundary between the cell wall and the cell cavity.

A: (playing) I don't understand that. Draw it.

Maria did.

50   Students and tutor turned to the text and examined the text's illustration. Maria kept reading from the text and Allison kept probing, saying it wasn't clear and could Maria put it in her own words. Allison explained that epithelial tissue helps push out bacteria.

A: What is germinal epithelial?

55   M: Is that the garbage?

A: (laughing) No. (Allison read from the text) "Sex cells must be released and come down for reproduction." (She drew a diagram of cells being released.) From where?

M: Epithelial.

60   A: (to Virginia) Could you put in your own words what we just said?

Virginia did so haltingly (and somewhat inaudibly).

Interpretation

Textual analysis of the preceding transcript illustrates a number of behaviors and interactions that are congruent with a student-centered learning model which uses expressive talk and writing as learning tools. In line 1 we see the tutor asking the students what they need to learn about, not what she is predetermined to teach. Though Maria replies that she is confused about "tissues," the tutor conveys to her that she already knows something about tissues (ll. 3-4) and is capable of explaining it to another student who was absent when the material was introduced. Line 5 indicates that the student does, indeed, know something about epithelial tissue: It is made up of flat sheets. Maria's summarizing thus keeps her at the center of her own learning and lessens her dependence on tutor/ teacher. In asking Maria to go to the board (l. 6), the tutor is further relinquishing control over the session and is putting the student in the role of teacher, an atypical role for ESL students in content classes. Though hesitant, Maria writes down the three focusing questions the group had generated the week before (ll. 13-15) With one exception, the student's grammatical errors are left uncorrected; they do not impede meaning. This reacquaintance with the material has enabled Maria to remember the function of epithelial tissue (ll. 19-20). When Maria reads from the textbook (l. 22), the tutor checks for comprehension by asking her to paraphrase the material. Maria, perhaps uncertain as to how to verbalize the material, draws a diagram. This process generates a new student-initiated question, "What you name the hair?" (l. 25). Though the tutor supplies the technical vocabulary (cilia), Maria is able to elaborate. She knows what cilia do and where they are located. The unfamiliar scientific vocabulary had eluded her, but by line 33, Maria is comfortable using the new word.

After Maria explains the function of epithelial tissue in the lungs (l. 33), the tutor asks Virginia to paraphrase what Maria has said. The tutor does not assume by Virginia's silence that she has understood everything. She is now being given the opportunity to make the knowledge her own by articulating the information herself. She takes an active role in the learning process.

Lines 39-42 illustrate the value of silence and a less dominant role for the teacher. Though initially Maria does not respond to Allison's question about other organs in which cilia are found, Allison bides her time (a painful experience, she later admits) and waits. Though lasting but a few seconds, the silence hangs heavily. Maria now offers "stomach, intestines" (l. 42). She has the satisfaction of supplying the information. By not providing all the answers, the tutor gives students opportunities to tap into their previous knowledge.

Throughout the transcript, it is evident that students are not permitted to hide behind textbook definitions or forced to speak in someone else's language. They are permitted to explore the concepts of the biology course as a precursor to acquiring the specific technical vocabulary. They are not repeating someone else's definitions. The learning always returns to them. The supportive group environment frees them to take chances while they learn to use the language of the biologist. Although this process is not without its frustrations, two pupils who *never* participated in the content course (corroborated by both tutor and teacher observation) are talking about material they thought they knew little about.

Evaluation

As part of its original FIPSE funding, the project involved a comprehensive evaluation plan. To measure the model's effectiveness in meeting its objectives, the researcher used several evaluation techniques. These included comparisons of class grades, consumer satisfaction questionnaires, instructor evaluations of the project, and interviews with project participants. (See Appendix B for sample evaluation instruments.) As indicated earlier, randomization was assured by predicating project participation on the availability of a common free period during which groups could meet. Other eligible ESL students who could not join a group thus became part of the control group.

The students' final grades in the content courses were used to measure the tutoring model's effects on increasing student comprehension of course material. This analysis was deemed useful because regardless of how they are derived, grades provide a realistic picture of how student learning is evaluated in the academic setting and offer students strong signals as to what constitutes "successful" learning. The final grade each student received (A,B,C,D, or F) was converted into the following numeric system: A = 4, B = 3, C = 2, D = 1, and F = 0. A further analysis of the difference in performance between the control and experimental groups was done by performing a t-test. This test, the recommended statistical form for the post-test-only control group design used here, enables one to determine whether differences between two sample means are significant and not attributable to chance. It provides an assessment of the magnitude and direction of any existing differences. The significance level selected was .05 to minimize the risk of committing a type I error (rejecting the null hypothesis when it is true).

Combined spring and fall semester grades during the academic years 1982-1984 revealed that students in the tutoring project received a final mean grade of 2.56 in their content courses while the control group received a score of 2.02. As hypothesized, students in the learning groups performed better than those in the control group, t (278) = 3.68; this is statistically significant at the .05 level. The scores suggest not only a higher degree of learning by project participants but also a wide margin of such learning.

Another strong indicator of project effectiveness was the percentage of high and low grades within the two populations. Project participants received 17 A's out of 114, a 15% rate. The control group received 11 A's out of 166 or a 7% rate. Thus, project participants received more than twice as many A's as did students in the control group. At the other end of the spectrum, the control group scored 31 F's out of 166, or a 19% rate, while project participants had only 2 F's out of 114 or under a 2% rate of failure. This quite unanticipated finding indicates that the model may be responsible for not only higher grades but also a stronger sense of accomplishment and satisfaction within this population. The implications of improved grade point averages are far-reaching and may affect student transferability to the senior colleges.

Table 1 summarizes our statistical findings.

Table 1: *Mean Class Grades by English Skills Level*

Course	n	Control	n	Experimental
		Fall 1982		
ENG 1300	36	2.25	16	2.81
ESL 1332	23	1.87	7	2.29
Total	59	2.10	23	2.65
$t(80) = 1.84$, significant at the .05 level				
		Spring 1983		
ENG 1300	24	2.29	24	2.42
ESL 1332	40	1.58	25	2.24
Total	64	1.84	49	2.33
$t(111) = 1.93$, significant at the .05 level				
		First-Year Results (1982-83)		
ENG 1300	60	2.27	40	2.58
ESL 1332	63	1.68	32	2.25
Total	123	2.00	72	2.43
$t(193) = 2.70$, significant at the .05 level				
		Fall 1983		
ENG 1300	14	2.14	10	2.90
ESL 1332	13	2.00	8	1.88
Total	27	2.07	18	2.44
Note. Significance could not be reached; sample size too small.				
		Spring 1984		
ENG 1300	8	2.50	14	3.14
ESL 1332	8	2.25	10	2.80
Total	16	2.38	24	3.00
Note. Significance could not be reached; sample size too small.				
		Second-Year Results (1983-84)		
ENG 1300	22	2.27	25	3.04
ESL 1332	21	2.10	18	2.40
Total	43	2.19	42	2.76
$t(83) = 2.80$, significant at the .05 level				
		Combined Two-Year Results (1982-84)		
ENG 1300	82	2.27	64	2.75
ESL 1332	84	1.78	50	2.32
Total	166	2.02	114	2.56
$t(278) = 3.68$, significant at the .05 level				

Student responses to the consumer satisfaction questionnaires (See Appendix B) indicated tremendous satisfaction with the project: 100% said the group increased their understanding of the content course and they would join a similar group again; 73% reported they felt comfortable expressing their opinions in the group; and 82% said they participated more in the group than in the content classroom.

Faculty evaluation of the project was overwhelmingly favorable. All instructors credited the project with improved student attendance, increased student participation in class, and improved student comprehension of course material. Specifically, 100% reported that students in groups increased their participation in class, and 67% felt that these students were able to speak more fluently about topics related to course material. In addition, 89% of the instructors responding said that students' understanding of course material improved as a result of group participation.

Project results extended well beyond the predictable. As noted, the comparison of high pass and failure rates between the control and experimental groups suggests a number of unanticipated consequences. In addition to providing students with greater self-esteem and transferability to senior colleges, higher rates of passing may also lead to lower rates of attrition within the college setting. We have already observed a higher rate of classroom attendance among project participants. Instructors with project participants confirmed that these students attended class regularly. This potentially significant effect on student attrition bears further study.

Summary

The great influx of nonnative speakers of English into American schools has made the language difficulties facing these students in content disciplines an issue of national importance. The project described here provides ESL educators and administrators with a tutoring model that enables adult, advanced ESL students in English-language content courses to improve their comprehension of course material. Successfully used for 4 years, the model continues to underscore the importance of expressive language, and especially talk, as a contributor to ESL student learning. The tutoring model also demonstrates that ESL students, like their native-speaking counterparts, can benefit from a language-rich, student-centered model that stresses the use of language for learning.

References

Barnes, D., Britton, J., & Rosen, H. (1969). *Language, the learner and the school.* Harmondsworth, England: Penguin.

Berthoff, A. E. (1981). *The making of meaning.* Montclair, NJ: Boynton/Cook.

Britton, J. (1970). *Language and learning.* Harmondsworth, England: Penguin.

Britton, J. (1982). Notes on a working hypothesis about writing. In G. M. Pradl (Ed.), *Prospect and retrospect.* (pp. 123-129). Montclair, NJ: Boynton/Cook.

Britton, J., Burgess, T., Martin, N., McLeod, A., & Rosen, H. (1975). *The development of writing abilities* (pp. 11-18). London: MacMillan Education.

Burgess, C., Burgess, T., Cartland, L., Chambers, R., Hedgeland, J., Levine, N., Mole, J., Newsome, B., Smith, H., & Torbe, M. (1973). *Understanding children writing.* Harmondsworth, England: Penguin.

Kelly, G. A. (1963). *A theory of personality.* New York: W. W. Norton & Co.

Martin, N., D'Arcy, P., Newton, B., & Parker, R. (1976). *Writing and learning across the curriculum* (pp. 11-16). London: Wardlock Educational.

Torbe, M., & Medway, P. (1981). *The climate for learning.* London: Wardlock Educational.

Appendix A

Tutor Training Materials

Arkin, A., & Shollar, B. (1982). *The tutor book.* New York: Longman.

Britton, J. (1971). What's the use? A schematic account of language function. *Education review, 23,* 205-219.

Draper, V. (1979). *Formative writing: Writing to assist learning in all subject areas.* Curriculum Publication No. 3: Bay Area Writing Project. Berkeley: University of California.

Emig, J. (1977). Writing as a mode of learning. *College Composition and Communication, 28,* 122-128.

Faigley, L., & Hansen, K. (1985). Learning to write in the social sciences. *College Composition and Communciation, 36,* 140-149.

Fulwiler, T. (1979). Journal-writing across the curriculum. *Classroom practices in teaching English 1979-1980: How to handle the paper load.* (pp. 15-22). Urbana, IL: NCTE

Herrington, A. J. (1981). Writing to learn: Writing across the disciplines. *College English, 43,* 379-387.

Irmscher, W. (1979). Writing as a way of learning and developing. *College Composition and Communication, 30,* 24-244.

Jacoby, J. (1983). Shall we talk to them in "English": The contributions of sociolinguists to training writing center personnel. *The Writing Center Journal, 4,* 1-14.

Knoblauch, C. H., & Brannon, L. (1983). Writing as learning through the curriculum. *College English, 45,* 465-474.

Krahnke, K. J., & Christison, M. A. (1983). Recent language research and some language teaching principles. *TESOL Quarterly, 17*, 625-649.

Krashen, S. (1982). *Principles and practice in second language acquisition.* Oxford, NY: Pergamon.

Mayher, J., & Lester, N. (1983). Putting learning first in writing to learn. *Language Arts, 60*, 717-722.

Mayher, J. S., Lester, N., & Pradl, G. M. (1983). *Learning to write/writing to learn.* Montclair, NJ: Boynton/Cook.

Raimes, A. (1983). Anguish as a second language? Remedies for composition teachers. In A. Freedman, I. Pringle, & J. Yalden (Eds.), *Learning to write: First language/second language.* (pp. 258-272). New York: Longman.

Sommers, N. (1982). Responding to student writing. *College Composition and Communication, 33*, 148-156.

Taylor, B. P. (1983). Teaching ESL: Incorporating a communicative student-centered component. *TESOL Quarterly, 17*, 69-88.

Torbe, M., & Medway, P. (1981). The climate for learning (pp. 40-45). London: Wardlock Educational.

Weiss, R. H. (1980). Writing in the total curriculum: A program for cross-disciplinary cooperation. In T. R. Donovan & B. W. McClelland (Eds.), *Eight approaches to teaching composition.* (pp. 133-149). Urbana, IL: NCTE.

Wotring, A. N., & Tierney, R. (1980). *Two studies of writing in high school science.* Classroom Research Study No. 5: Bay Area Writing Project. Berkeley: University of California.

Zamel, V. (1982). Writing: The process of discovering meaning. *TESOL Quarterly, 16*, 195-209.

Appendix B

Evaluation Instruments

(Pre-form)
Hostos Community College, City University of New York
Linda Hirsch, Project Coordinator/Tutor Coordinator
FIPSE Project: "The Learning of a Discipline"

In order that we may evaluate the success of this project, we would appreciate your answering the following questions. Please do not put your name on the paper. Thank you for your cooperation.

I. Background Information

   1. English composition course you are taking this semester

   2. How many courses are you taking this semester?

   3. How many of the courses you are taking are taught in English?

   4. Please list the courses you are taking in English.

II. Below are a number of statements about _____.
Please indicate whether you agree or disagree with each statement by circling one number to the right of each statement that best expresses your opinion.

	Strongly Agree	Agree	Disagree	Strongly Disagree
1. I understand the class lectures.	1	2	3	4
2. I understand the homework assignments.	1	2	3	4
3. I ask questions in class whenever I want.	1	2	3	4
4. I feel comfortable joining in class discussions.	1	2	3	4
5. The English used by the instructor is too difficult for me.	1	2	3	4
6. The English used in the text is too difficult for me.	1	2	3	4
7. I frequently participate in this class.	1	2	3	4
8. I could write an essay in English based on this class.	1	2	3	4

III. Please rate your ability with regard to the following writing skills on a scale of Superior to Poor. Circle the number next to each statement that best expresses your ability.

	Superior			Poor
1. Overall writing quality	1	2	3	4
2. Organization	1	2	3	4
3. State a main idea	1	2	3	4
4. Support my main idea	1	2	3	4
5. Choose words that say what I mean	1	2	3	4
6. Revise my ideas	1	2	3	4
7. Revise my sentences	1	2	3	4
8. Judge my own writing	1	2	3	4
9. Use correct grammar	1	2	3	4
10. Use correct punctuation	1	2	3	4
11. Use correct spelling	1	2	3	4

Appendix B

Evaluation Instruments

(Post-Form)
Hostos Community College, City University of New York
Linda Hirsch, Project Coordinator/Tutor Coordinator
FIPSE Project: "The Learning of a Discipline"

In order that we may evaluate the success of this project, we would appreciate your answering the following questions. Please do not put your name on the paper. Thank you for your cooperation.

I. Background Information

1. English composition course you are taking this semester

2. Subject of Tutor Group

II. Directions: Below are a number of statements about the tutor group you have been attending this semester. Please indicate whether you agree or disagree with each statement by circling one number to the right of each statement that best expresses your opinion.

	Strongly Agree 1	Agree 2	Disagree 3	Strongly Disagree 4
1. The tutor group increased my understanding of the course materials.	1	2	3	4
2. The tutor group helped me improve my writing skills.	1	2	3	4
3. I didn't feel comfortable talking in the group.	1	2	3	4
4. I expressed my opinions in the group.	1	2	3	4
5. I expect to get a better grade because of the tutor group.	1	2	3	4
6. I liked the way the group was run.	1	2	3	4
7. I felt I had a responsibility to contribute to group discussions.	1	2	3	4
8. I felt I had a responsibility to regularly attend group meetings.	1	2	3	4
9. I participated more in the tutor group than in class.	1	2	3	4
10. I would participate in a group like this again.	1	2	3	4

III. Comments:

Appendix B

Evaluation Instruments

Hostos Community College, City University of New York
"The Learning of a Discipline"
TO: Professor
FROM: Linda Hirsch, Project Coordinator
DATE:
RE: Project Evaluations

The following students from your _____ class have been
participating in our tutorial program.

To help evaluate the tutoring your students have received, we are
asking you to take a few moments to complete the following questionnaire. Please circle one response to the right of each statement.

1. In general, have the students' understand-   yes no don't know
   ing of the course content been improved?

2. Have these students increased their   yes no don't know
   participation in your class?

3. Are these students now able to write more   yes no don't know
   fluently about topics which pertain to
   your course?

4. Are these students now able to speak more   yes no don't know
   fluently about topics which pertain to
   your course?

5. In general, did these students attend your   yes no don't know
   class regularly?

6. Were you pleased with the tutors'   yes no don't know
   relationships to you and your class?

7. Are there other ways in which the tutors   yes no don't know
   might have served you or your class? If so,
   please elaborate.

_____

_____

8. Please feel free to make any further comments on the tutorial
   project below.

   _____

   _____

Once again, we thank you for your continued support this semester.

About the Author

Linda Hirsch is an assistant professor of ESL/English and Director of the Writing Center at Hostos Community College, CUNY. She is currently director of the language-across-the-curriculum program described here and has received a FIPSE Award, a FIPSE Dissemination Award, and a CUNY Retention Exemplary Model Program Award for her work in this area. A frequent presenter at national and regional conferences including TESOL and NCTE, she has published articles on her work with ESL students in content courses and the training of tutors in CUNY *Resource*, the TESOL *IDIOM*, and other CUNY publications. She is also a coauthor of *Worksheet: A Business-Based Writing and Grammar Guide*, published by Prentice-Hall in 1987.

Language and/or Content?
Principles and Procedures for Materials Development in an Adjunct Course

Ellen Guyer

Pat Wilcox Peterson

Macalester College

Abstract

Language teachers generally agree that the primary goal of the language classroom is to provide opportunities for students to become proficient in the target language. However, the vehicle for providing this practice is not so easily determined. This article proposes a course model which focuses on the teaching of content as a means for developing language fluency. Specifically, the adjunct course model, wherein a language course is paired with a course from another academic area, provides students with an opportunity to learn the concepts and terminology of one academic discipline while meeting their needs for language and study skill development. The language course concentrates on helping students identify what they have not understood from the text or lectures of the content course and assists them in acquiring this missing information. Exercises integrate the language skills and develop approaches to studying content which can transfer to other academic courses.

Language and/or Content?
Principles and Procedures for Materials Development in an Adjunct Course

Issues in Course Design

Choosing Appropriate Subject Content

In any college preparatory ESL class, there is a tension between teaching language skills and teaching academic subject content. Having rejected the grammatical syllabus and the study of language as form, the profession has gone on, through a series of needs assessments, to teach the use of language in the communicative settings that our students are most likely to encounter (Krashen, 1982; Richterich & Chancerel, 1978; Widdowson, 1978). As a result, academically oriented ESL classes now outwardly resemble other subject classrooms in the type of language activity the students are asked to perform (Fein & Baldwin, 1986).

Yet the ESL syllabus is still primarily a language syllabus. As language teachers, we are generally less concerned that our students master specific subject content than we are that they attain a certain level of language proficiency. The content is interesting only insofar as it can be used for the performance of communicative tasks. At this point we raise a general issue in course design: Is the choice of content for language courses really of little consequence as long as the learners are involved in language practice that is appropriate to their skill level?

Models for Combining Language and Content

Courses in which primary emphasis is given to the development of one or more language skills are known as skills-based courses. When the sequence of lessons in the syllabus is not determined by the language skills to be learned, but rather by the content itself, we call the course content-based. Examples of content-based courses are sheltered courses and adjunct courses.

Many skills-based ESL courses are nonspecialized in content in that selections used for reading and listening passages range across several disciplines. In ESL courses such as Advanced Composition or Critical Reading, the language skill is at the core, and the content of the course is chosen more or less arbitrarily to provide practice in that skill. Reading assignments within the span of one term may include social history, philosophy, biology, psychology, and fiction (Behrens & Rosen, 1984; Zimbardo & Stevens, 1985).

One advantage of this plan is that eventually everyone's special interest is more likely to be met, and students are provided with an excellent introduction to the thought processes required for a liberal arts education. Because the skills-based ESL course is organized around the content of many disciplines, it can serve an important function in orienting international students to their study in the United States and in providing for discussions of the disciplinary conventions of different discourse communities.

While a general ESL course can provide a glimpse into various disciplines, it can not provide the depth of information and types of analysis in one field which are necessary to develop the cognitive skills required for a specific academic course. A typical college course builds on itself as the semester progresses, presenting a set of principles and ideas and technical terminology. Learning is cumulative; students are asked throughout the term to remember and to use information which shows deep and complex relationships. Students are asked to become socialized into the culture of the discipline, to use its tools of analysis, and to think like a specialist. To be proficient in an academic discipline is to have a sense of the discipline as it unfolds through time.

An alternative course model for students who are preparing for academic study would require students to spend an entire semester learning the concepts and terminology of one academic discipline and building the specific language skills needed to do academic work. The adjunct course in ESL is designed to build both linguistic and academic skills by allowing students to participate in a college level course.

The Adjunct Course

Curricular Design

At Macalester College we offer an ESL language and study skills course which is paired with an academic course, Human Geography. Students are targeted for these classes upon completion of the required advanced level ESL courses, Advanced Composition and Critical Reading or if their scores on our ESL Placement Battery exempt them from ESL courses but indicate the desirability of some further language assistance. Although a few members of the class possess advanced English skills, these students still need assistance adjusting to the academic milieu. For many new students the ESL-Geography pair represents their first experience with an academic course taught in English. The students come from a variety of countries and intend to major in different subjects.

Geography was chosen as the academic field for the adjunct course because of the nature of the discipline and for pragmatic reasons. Human geography provides a good introduction to modes of thought in the social sciences, and it uses some of the quantitative tools of the natural sciences. At our college, geography has an international focus appropriate for ESL students. Perhaps most important, our colleagues in the geography department are cooperative and creative teachers, willing to put in the extra time for consultation required by the adjunct course. This is an important pragmatic consideration in a curricular model involving teamwork or team teaching.

The geography course is not a sheltered course with enrollment limited to international students so that the professor will alter his presentation and simplify his speaking style (Edwards, Wesche, Krashen, Clement, & Kruidenier, 1984; Krashen, 1980). Rather, both American and international students are present in a regular introductory geography class which contains little or no modification of input. This curricular design allows students to experience the typical rhythm of the classroom: presentation of material, review, testing, research, development of individual projects, and final examinations.

Language support is given to supplement the course: An ESL teacher attends geography lectures and follows the reading assignments. After the lectures she meets with international students for an hour of intensive work in listening comprehension, vocabulary development, critical reading, note-taking, library work, writing practice, and class discussion.

Balancing Language and Content

In the adjunct course model, we have solved the problem of which content to teach; however, the tension between content and language skills does not disappear. Students sense the importance of content in the geography lectures and text. Accordingly, they may be much more interested in using the ESL study skills hour to review geography content than to engage in skill-building activities which do not seem to offer an immediate reward.

The ESL instructor must resist pressure to dwell on content. She may plan a lesson on understanding vocabulary from context and find instead she is repeating the day's geography lecture, in simplified form. Digressions like this endanger the authenticity of the course, as a nonspecialist's simplifications of the lectures often distort course content. The ultimate sources of authority are the text and the professor, and the ESL teacher's role is to teach students to get the information they need from these sources. Exercises are designed to facilitate this process of identifying what a student has not understood and how to retrieve the missing information.

We have decided to handle this language/content conflict by addressing students' immediate needs for content mastery first and then by shifting the focus of the course to language and study skills that make students more independent.

Three Phases to Academic Proficiency

Our experience teaching adjunct courses has made us sympathetic to the students' need to understand subject content from the outset. Students in a fast-moving introductory course simply must understand the geography lectures and the textbook if they are to keep step with the class during the critical period of adjustment. During this phase the ESL instructor does well to provide maximum support for processing information in the geography course. Exercise types are closely related to the language found in the lectures and texts. Students receive study guides, reading questions, lecture outlines, and transcripts of the lectures. In the first third of the course, the teacher needs to encourage the students, explain the nature of the task, and help them process the geographic content. If the instructor continues to process the material for students, they fail to learn the study skills needed for independence in later courses. It does not help them to pass the geography course but to have no transferable survival skills. Therefore, in the middle third of the study skills course the instructor requires students to prepare notes, outlines, and study questions themselves.

In the last phase of the course, students are asked to do library work and outside reading which go beyond the requirements of the geography course. They relate the terms and concepts learned in geography to current issues and events reported in newspapers and magazine articles. Class time is devoted to oral research reports, peer editing of first drafts of papers, and class discussion. Students are required to analyze, synthesize, and evaluate information independently as the semester progresses.

Principles of Materials Development

There are two general areas of concern in materials development: principles which govern the selection of the content to be taught and principles which guide us in the selection and sequencing of skills. ESL lessons in the adjunct course should be based on significant content material and should follow a progression of task types from simple to difficult throughout the semester.

Recognizing Important Subject Content

Both American and international students need to determine how much of the lecture and reading material is really important and what level of detail the professor expects them to learn. The introductory geography course includes more case studies, illustrations, and examples than students are able to master if they insist on remembering material at a fine level of detail. The great amount of illustrative material presented in the American classroom is there to emphasize larger trends and concepts, not to be memorized as an encyclopedia of facts. Faced with these demands, students who have always relied on memorization are at a disadvantage, and students who have learned to abstract the main idea of a selection are in a stronger position. The ability to recognize abstract ideas and thought patterns may be less developed in certain groups of international students than in Americans because of the different study habits and cognitive styles which characterize the academic cultures of their countries (Brew, 1980; Brislin, 1981; Dudley-Evans, 1980).

In our selection of content material for the adjunct course, we have come to rely on a typical device used in the discourse of geographers: explanatory models based on historical patterns, which are used to explain general phenomena in human society. These models show the students how the professor tends to think, what constitutes proof of an idea in geography, and how an argument is built. Such metacognitive strategies are part of what is being taught when the professor says "Now I want you to think like a geographer." (See Appendix A for an illustration of such a model and the accompanying language exercise.)

Explanatory models are often presented in the form of a graph or visual aid, which makes them ideal for pedagogic language exercises of the information transfer type (Widdowson, 1978). The visual aid serves as a language elicitation device when students are asked to practice their productive skills of speaking or writing. When students are given a written or spoken text, they can then construct a visual diagram to show that they have understood the material; this is an exercise in the receptive skills of reading and listening. Careful reading of graphs and familiarity with the language of graphs are two important language skills for all the natural and social sciences.

Sequencing Skills and Activities

The second area of concern in materials development is the sequencing of skills and activities that allows students to progress along the lines defined elsewhere in certain linguistic and cognitive hierarchies (Bloom, Eglehart, Furst, Hill, & Krathwohl, 1956; 1956; Revised ACTFL Proficiency Guidelines, 1986). We provide maximum support at the beginning of the course, and as students learn, we withdraw some support until they can function quite well by themselves. Examples of such supportive, lower- level tasks are those which provide students with more text and ask them to provide less; those which allow students several opportunities to hear or read the text before solving a problem; those which follow a familiar model or use a familiar context; and those which call for factual comprehension and restatement.

Conversely, higher order tasks are those which ask students to provide most of the text; which give fewer opportunities for the students to read the text or to hear it repeated; or which require students to apply information and concepts to novel settings.

In general, we favor tasks that require students to actively manipulate given information to solve a problem; tasks that require the integration of listening, speaking, reading, and writing; and tasks that appeal to a variety of learning styles (Oxford-Carpenter, 1985).

Language Skill Goals and Exercise Types

The syllabus for the course claims that "at the end of the course, students will have better skills for academic work and will be able to use these skills in all their academic subjects." The following language improvement goals for each skill are given with a summary of exercise types. Samples of selected exercises are included in Appendix A.

Listening Comprehension

Listening exercises focus on the ability to follow the main ideas of a lecture, to understand supporting examples and nonverbal information, to take useful notes, to determine what has not been understood, and to identify a way to clarify that information. Examples of such an exercise include:

Incomplete outline/study guide. Study guides highlight the structure and organization of the lecture as well as its factual content. Students may listen to the video segment as many times as they need in order to get the information.

Listening with lecture transcripts. Students are asked to pick out transition words and discourse organizers as they read and listen. This helps make the connection between the written and the spoken word and may be particularly good for weak listeners (Lebauer, 1984).

Abbreviations for note-taking. Students learn the most frequent content vocabulary of the discipline and develop a personal system of abbreviations for note-taking.

Use of nonverbal devices. Students copy visuals, graphs, and other nonverbal information from the board. They are advised to include all labels and other accompanying prose which explain the significance of the visual (Widdowson, 1978).

Group outlining exercises. After an initial phase of guided note-taking, students begin to listen to lectures without use of prepared study guides. They work together as a class to prepare a lecture outline. This is a cumulative skill exercise requiring the use of abbreviations, recognition of the speaker's intent, and knowledge of the general organization of the lecture as well as familiarity with the ideas and vocabulary.

Reading

Reading exercises develop the ability to follow the main idea of a passage, to read selectively for information which answers specific questions, to read different types of prose, such as novels or newspaper articles, and to increase the rate of reading to a speed which permits efficient academic performance. Examples of exercises include:

Chapter outlines and study guides. These are prepared initially under the direction of the teacher using the SQ3R method (survey, question, read, review, and recite). Students are expected to take over the preparation of the outlines themselves. These guides emphasize the main ideas of the passage.

Scanning questions. Students must review the reading material quickly to find specific pieces of information.

Paraphrasing and summary writing. After reading a selection, students summarize the content in their own words.

Graph reading. Prepared questions force students to focus on charts, maps, and other textual aids.

Speed-reading exercises. Students are taught to preread each article and to build their anticipation and prediction skills by forming prereading questions. They learn to distinguish critical information from less relevant material.

Vocabulary from context. New technical terms are often defined in context; students practice recognizing cues that point to the special language of definitions.

Composition

Composition tasks work on the ability to summarize and paraphrase information, to synthesize information from a variety of sources, to apply previously learned concepts to new situations, and to write under time pressure short answers to essay test items. Such exercises include:

Summarizing lecture notes. Students discuss the day's geography lecture, the teacher writes an outline on the blackboard, and students then write summaries based on the outline. This not only reinforces and clarifies information from the lecture, but also allows students to check the accuracy of their notes.

Summarizing text chapters. Students are often asked to write one-page summaries of the main ideas of the assigned chapters. This is particularly useful for developing the skill of paraphrasing.

Dicto-comps. The teacher chooses a short, interesting paragraph incorporating the vocabulary and structures that have been used in the geography unit. Students listen carefully to the paragraph as a whole to get an idea of the content before they begin to write. After the teacher reads the paragraph a number of times, students work for five or ten minutes to complete the paragraph from memory, as close to the original form as they can reproduce.

Information transfer exercises (Widdowson, 1978). Students are asked to write short essays explaining the information found in a chart or graph.

Time-pressured writing. After anticipating questions likely to be included in an exam, students draft answers to four or five of those questions in a limited amount of time. Their responses are then scored in class and students discuss better ways to manage their time and preparation.

Essays and term papers. Students are asked to analyze various geographical problems by referring to articles in an anthology. They are also required to write a research paper on a topic of current interest in the field of geography.

Speaking

Speaking exercises enable students to ask questions for clarification of information, to contribute actively to class discussions and problem solving activities, to use interview techniques to obtain information from native speakers of English, and to present oral reports based on reading or research. Examples of such exercises are:

Lecture summary. Students summarize orally the content of the day's lecture.

Information gap exchange. Students work in pairs, describing maps or visuals so that one student gives information about the visual that the other student lacks (Brown & Yule, 1983).

Interviews. Students interview native speakers to discover what kinds of mental maps and concepts of regionalization their American counterparts have.

Prereading brainstorming. Students summarize their background information and understanding of a certain topic, idea, or region of the world. This prepares them for the introduction of a new topic. It also illustrates how their cultural backgrounds may have given them an understanding of the subject which differs from the American students' or the lecturer's understanding of the subject.

Oral reports. Students prepare an oral report on a chapter or an article they have read.

Small group discussions. Students talk about geographic problems, applying geographic principles in their problem solving.

Course Evaluation and Student Progress

Evidence of the success of the adjunct course model comes from data on student performance on geography tests, comments from geography professors, and student evaluations. Clearly, the course has accomplished one of its stated goals, to give students better skills for academic work. Improved skills for adjunct course students are evident in a comparison of students in three language proficiency groups (see Appendix B). Performance on unit tests throughout the semester was measured for American students who are native speakers of English (NS), for nonnative speaker students with no language handicap who did not take the language support course (NNS, no "bridge" course), and for nonnative speakers who had the language support and skills course (NNS, "bridge").

As might be expected, initial success on the geography unit tests was directly related to the level of language proficiency. Throughout the semester, all groups improved in their ability to score well on geography tests. The results for all semesters, however, show that language proficiency alone is no guarantor of academic success. The NNS group with benefit of the study skills class was able to pass the NNS group with superior language proficiency and in some semesters to approach the average score for native speakers. This supports our view that academic success is partially dependent on understanding the conventions and expectations of the specific academic culture and discipline.

Comments from geography professors indicate that the adjunct course has a dramatic effect on retention rate; previously, before the addition of the language support course, most international students dropped or failed the geography course.

Student evaluations are mixed. While most students felt their language and study skills improved, some were unhappy that geography was the only choice available for an adjunct course. This problem will be solved as we develop other adjunct course alternatives in humanities, math, and natural sciences.

We do not yet know how well the students' academic skills have transferred to other courses, but a long-term study is planned to answer this question. The group of international students who have had the adjunct courses will be followed through their four years of study at Macalester and compared to the rest of the international student population for grade point average, number of courses dropped, and number of semesters required to complete the degree.

Summary

The adjunct course model provides students with a challenging and helpful experience as they make the transition from study of language to use of language in the study of other academic disciplines. The close relationship of content, language, and study skills introduces students to the thought patterns of American academic culture in general and to the methods of a specific discipline. This article has provided a set of principles and procedures for materials development which could be used in various subjects to create adjunct courses.

The materials for the adjunct course were developed under the support of a faculty development and curriculum grant from the Bush Foundation, and we are grateful to the Bush Foundation and to Macalester College for this support. We gratefully acknowledge the help and expertise of our subject area professors in geography, Dr. David Lanegran and Dr. Jerry Pitzl, who teach Human Geography and act as consultants in the project.

'S

Behrens, ...ding across the curriculum. Boston:
Littl...
Bloom, B. .... , rurst, E. J., Hill, W. H., & Krathwohl, D. R.
(1956). .... educational objectives. The classification of educational
goals. I.   .JK I: Cognitive domain. New York: Longmans Green.
Brew, A. (1980). Responses of overseas students to differing teaching styles. In ELT
documents 109: Study modes and academic development of overseas students.
(pp. 115-125). London: British Council.
Brislin, R. (1981). Learning styles. In Learning across cultures. (pp. 128-135).
Washington, DC: National Association of Foreign Student Affairs.
Broek, J. & Webb, J. (1978). A geography of mankind. New York: McGraw-Hill.
Brown, G. & Yule, G. (1983). Teaching the spoken language: An approach based on
the analysis of conversational English. Cambridge: Cambridge University
Press.
Dudley-Evans, A. (1980). Study modes and students from the Middle East. In ELT
documents 109: Study modes and academic development of overseas students.
(pp. 91-103). London: British Council.
Edwards, H., Wesche, M., Krashen, S. D., Clement, R., & Kruidenier, B. (1984).
Second-language acquisition through subject matter learning: A study of shel-
tered psychology classes at the University of Ottawa. The Canadian Modern
Language Review, 41, 268-282.
Fein, D., & Baldwin, R. (1986). Content-based curriculum design in advanced levels
of an intensive ESL program. English for Foreign Students in English-speaking
Countries Interest Section Newsletter, 4, 1-3. Washington, DC: TESOL.
Krashen, S. D. (1982). Principles and practice in second language acquisition.
Oxford: Oxford University Press.
Krashen, S. D. (1980). The theoretical and practical relevance of simplified codes in
second language acquisition. In R. Scarcerella and S. Krashen (Eds.), Research
in second language acquisition. Rowley, MA: Newbury House.
Lanegran, D. A. Geography in everyday life. Unpublished manuscript.
Lebauer, R. S. (1984). Using lecture transcripts in EAP lecture comprehension
courses. TESOL Quarterly, 18, 41-54.
Oxford-Carpenter, P. (1985). A new taxonomy of second language learning strate-
gies. Washington, DC: ERIC Clearinghouse on Languages and Linguistics.
Revised ACTFL Proficiency Guidelines. (1986). The ACTFL Foreign Language
Education Series. Lincolnwood, IL: National Textbook.
Richterich, R., & Chancerel, J. L. (1978). Identifying the needs of adults learning a
foreign language. Strasbourg: Council for Cultural Cooperation of the Council
of Europe.
Widdowson, H. G. (1979). Explorations in applied linguistics. Oxford: Oxford Uni-
versity Press.
Widdowson, H. G. (1978). Teaching language as communication. Oxford: Oxford
University Press.
Zimbardo, R., & Stevens, M. (1985). Across the curriculum: Thinking, reading, and
writing. New York: Longman.

Appendix A

Sample Exercises

Graph interpretation: the demographic transition.

One of the most important topics of the Human Geography course is world population trends. The model of the European demographic transition from the 18th to the 20th century is presented to illustrate the effects of modernization, urbanization, and medical advances on population growth. The professor then speculates as to whether the patterns of this demographic transition are universal processes which can be seen to operate in societies in different places, times, and under different types of social organization. He attempts to apply the model to contemporary Third World countries or to Socialist block countries and asks the students to judge whether the model provides an appropriate interpretation of the geographic facts.

Our instructional plan proceeds along these lines: First we make sure that the students can handle the graphs, charts, facts, and trends completely. They are asked to describe a graph about the demographic transition and to interpret its message. Then we ask them to examine whether the model applies to the situation in other countries. They must skim the chapter reading (Lanegran, in press) and copy the relevant information into a fact sheet. For this exercise, the order of information in the text is not exactly the same as the layout of the fact sheet, so the students must evaluate and organize the information themselves. Finally, the students are asked to evaluate the usefulness of the model as a universal process, using specific examples from their reading.

The Demographic Transition

Write at least one paragraph to explain the ideas conveyed in the graph below, which describes the demographic transition. In your essay, include the following information:
1. Describe what is measured on the vertical and horizontal axes,
2. Describe the birth rate, death rate, and rate of population growth for each stage,
3. Tell what historical factors caused the birth rate and death rate to be as they were in each stage.

DEMOGRAPHIC TRANSITION IN ENGLAND AND WALES

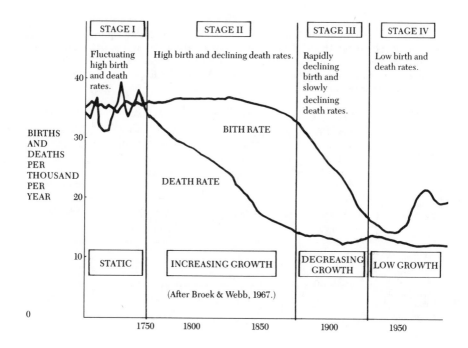

(After Broek & Webb, 1967.)

Organize the information in Lanegran #3 and fill in the chart below. For some countries you will be able to supply the actual dates for each stage of the demographic transition. Some countries have not yet reached the third and fourth stages of the transition; note this on the chart. Some countries seem to be going through a demographic transition similar to the mode in Western Europe, but at a different rate and for different reasons.

Composition Topic

Write a coherent essay in which you answer the following question. You may use the reading chart to help you organize your answer.

CAN THE DEMOGRAPHIC TRANSITION BE APPLIED TO AREAS OUTSIDE THE INDUSTRIALIZED WORLD?

STUDY GUIDE, LANEGRAN CH. 3 CASE STUDIES IN POPULATION

Organize the information in Lanegran #3 and fill in the chart below. For some countries you will be able to supply the actual dates for each stage of the demographic transition. Some countries have not yet reached the third and fourth stages of the transition; note this on the chart. Some countries seem to be going through a demographic transition similar to the mode in Western Europe, but at a different rate and for different reasons.

COUNTRY	STAGE 1 (High CBR High CDR Stable Population)	STAGE 2 (Stable CBR Falling CDR High rate of population growth)	STAGE 3 (Falling CBR Low stable CDR Rate of population growth is slowing)	STAGE 4 (Low CBR Low CDR Growth low or negative)
Western Europe	When? Why?	When? Why?	When? Why?	When? Why?
U.S.A.				
Latin America				
Africa				
Arab World				
China				
U.S.S.R.				
Japan				

Look at the summary of information which you produced in your chart. Does it seem that all 8 of the areas are following the same path of development as Western Europe? If there are differences in the relationship of the birth and death rates, what could explain these differences?

Do you think that Africa, Latin America, and the Arab World will eventually go through the 4 stages of the demographic transition? Will they take the same amount of time as Western Europe did? How is the situation in the world different now from the situation when Western Europe went through the transition?

Appendix B

Course Evaluation and Student Progress

Improvement on Geography unit tests through the term

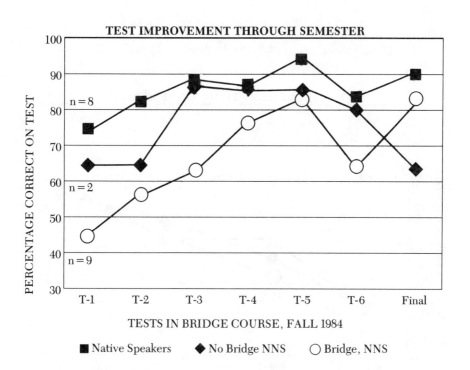

TEST IMPROVEMENT THROUGH SEMESTER

PERCENTAGE CORRECT ON TEST

TESTS IN BRIDGE COURSE, FALL 1984

■ Native Speakers   ◆ No Bridge NNS   ○ Bridge, NNS

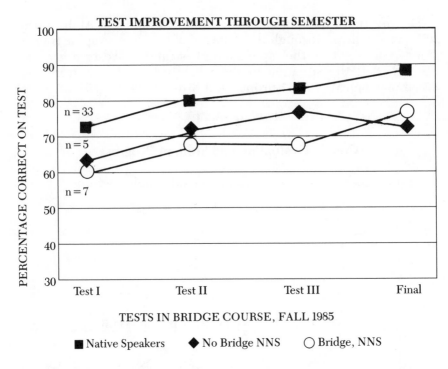

TEST IMPROVEMENT THROUGH SEMESTER

PERCENTAGE CORRECT ON TEST

n = 33

n = 5

n = 7

TESTS IN BRIDGE COURSE, FALL 1985

■ Native Speakers   ◆ No Bridge NNS   ○ Bridge, NNS

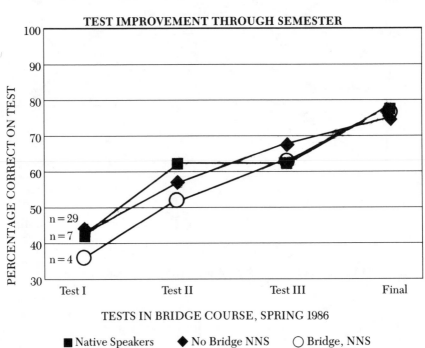

TEST IMPROVEMENT THROUGH SEMESTER

PERCENTAGE CORRECT ON TEST

n = 29

n = 7

n = 4

TESTS IN BRIDGE COURSE, SPRING 1986

■ Native Speakers   ◆ No Bridge NNS   ○ Bridge, NNS

About the Authors

Ellen D. Guyer has been teaching ESL at Macalester College for the past ten years. Prior to this she taught EFL in the Peace Corps in Gabon, Africa. She earned a MA in TESOL from Teachers College at Columbia University in 1976 and is currently pursuing a PhD degree in Educational Pyschology at the University of Minnesota. Ms. Guyer has presented extensively at TESOL conventions and has published articles on cultural orientation programs for international students. Her research interests include learning and teaching styles and the cognitive strategies involved in reading and writing.

Pat Wilcox Peterson is an instructor in the departments of Linguistics/ESL and German at Macalester College. Her degrees are in Language Education (MAT Yale, 1969; MA New York University, 1972; ABD University of Minnesota, 1986). Ms. Peterson has authored five textbooks for ESL, has served as an academic expert for the USIA in Sri Lanka and Turkey, and has taught in Yugoslavia. Her research interests include information processing strategies in listening comprehension and specific purpose language teaching. As a teacher educator, she is interested in teaching language through content areas.